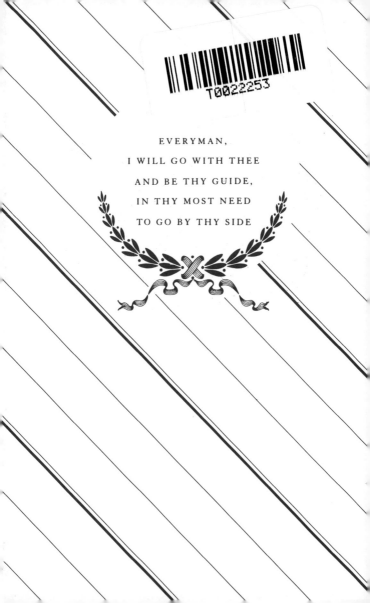

EVERYMAN,
I WILL GO WITH THEE
AND BE THY GUIDE,
IN THY MOST NEED
TO GO BY THY SIDE

EVERYMAN'S LIBRARY
POCKET POETS

NO PLACE LIKE HOME

POEMS

EDITED BY
JANE HOLLOWAY

EVERYMAN'S LIBRARY
POCKET POETS

Alfred A. Knopf New York London Toronto

THIS IS A BORZOI BOOK
PUBLISHED BY ALFRED A. KNOPF

This selection by Jane Holloway
first published in Everyman's Library, 2022
Copyright © 2022 by Everyman's Library

A list of acknowledgments to copyright owners appears
at the back of this volume.

everymanslibrary.com
www.everymanslibrary.co.uk

ISBN 978-0-593-32129-4 (US)
978-1-84159-825-3 (UK)

A CIP catalogue record for this book is available
from the British Library

Typography by Peter B. Willberg

Typeset in the UK by Input Data Services Ltd, Isle Abbotts,
Somerset

Printed and bound in Germany
by GGP Media GmbH, Pössneck

CONTENTS

TOWN AND COUNTRY

THE PEOPLE NEXT DOOR

ENTERTAINING

DECEPTIVELY SPACIOUS

SAFE AS HOUSES

This is the true nature of home – it is the place of Peace; the shelter, not only from all injury, but from all terror, doubt, and division. In so far as it is not this, it is not home; so far as the anxieties of the outer life penetrate into it, and the inconsistently-minded, unknown, unloved, or hostile society of the outer world is allowed by either husband or wife to cross the threshold, it ceases to be home; it is then only a part of that outer world which you have roofed over, and lighted fire in.

JOHN RUSKIN, *Sesame and Lilies*

To be happy at home is the ultimate result of all ambition, the end to which every enterprise and labour tends, and of which every desire prompts the prosecution.

SAMUEL JOHNSON, *The Rambler*

'COME LIVE WITH ME': SETTING UP HOME

The little house ceased to be a glorified bower, but it became a home and the young couple soon felt that it was a change for the better.

LOUISA MAY ALCOTT

COLIN AND LUCY

Colin: Gentle maid, consent to be
A rural bride, and dwell with me,
Where the woodland warblers sing
Songs of love, to hail the spring –
Where sweet wild flowers scent the gale
Round my cottage of the vale.

The jess'mine dark with snowy gems,
Scatter'd o'er its bending stems;
And the woodbine's tendrils twine
With the blushing eglantine,
To form a rural bower for thee –
Quit for these thy liberty.

Lucy: Shepherd, tho' thy song be sweet,
And thy cottage is complete,
Yet, should I consent to be
A rural bride, and dwell with thee,
Shall good-humour still prevail
In thy cottage of the vale?

Say, shall never frowns or strife
Make me rue a married life?
Wilt thou constant be and kind,
And as now to love inclin'd?
Else to me would sweeter be
A single life and liberty.

ISABELLA LICKBARROW (1784–1847)

THE BLISSFUL BOWER
From *Paradise Lost*

Thus talking, hand in hand alone they passed
On to their blissful bower; it was a place
Chosen by the sovereign planter, when he framed
All things to man's delightful use; the roof
Of thickest covert was inwoven shade,
Laurel and myrtle, and what higher grew
Of firm and fragrant leaf; on either side
Acanthus, and each odorous bushy shrub,
Fenced up the verdant wall; each beauteous flower,
Iris all hues, roses, and jessamine,
Reared high their flourished heads between,
    and wrought
Mosaic; under foot the violet,
Crocus, and hyacinth, with rich inlay
Broidered the ground, more coloured than with stone
Of costliest emblem; other creature here,
Beast, bird, insect, or worm, durst enter none;
Such was their awe of man. In shadier bower
More sacred and sequestered, though but feigned,
Pan or Sylvanus never slept, nor nymph
Nor Faunus haunted. Here, in close recess,
With flowers, garlands, and sweet-smelling herbs,
Espousèd Eve decked her first nuptial bed.

YES, I'LL MARRY YOU, MY DEAR

Yes, I'll marry you, my dear, and here's the reason why:
So I can push you out of bed when the baby starts
    to cry,
And if we hear a knocking and it's creepy and it's late,
I hand you the torch you see and *you* investigate.

Yes, I'll marry you, my dear, you may not apprehend it,
But when the tumble-drier goes it's you that has to
    mend it,
You have to face the neighbour, should our labrador
    attack him,
And if a drunkard fondles me, it's *you* that has to
    whack him.

Yes, I'll marry you, my dear, you're virile and
    you're lean,
My house is like a pigsty, *you* can help to keep it clean,
That little sexy dinner which you served by
    candlelight,
As I just do chipolatas, you can cook it every night!

It's you who has to work the drill and put up
    curtain track,
And when I've got the PMT it's you who gets the flak,
I *do* see great advantages, but none of them for you,
And so before you see the light, I do I do I do!

PAM AYRES (1947−)

THE FINISHED HOUSE

In the finished house a flame is brought to the hearth.
Then a table, between door and window
Where a stranger will eat before the men of
  the house.
A bed is laid in a secret corner
For the three agonies – love, birth, death –
That are made beautiful with ceremony.
The neighbours come with gifts –
A set of cups, a calendar, some chairs.
A fiddle is hung at the wall.
A girl puts lucky salt in a dish.
The cupboard will have its loaf and bottle,
  come winter.
On the seventh morning
One spills water of blessing over the threshold.

THE CABBAGE

You have rented an apartment.
You come to this enclosure with physical relief,
your heavy body climbing the stairs in the dark,
the hall bulb burned out, the landlord
of Greek extraction and possibly a fatalist.
In the apartment leaning against one wall,
your daughter's painting of a large frilled cabbage
against a dark sky with pinpoints of stars.
The eager vegetable, opening itself
as if to eat the air, or speak in cabbage
language of the meanings within meanings;
while the points of stars hide their massive
violence in the dark upper half of the painting.
You can live with this.

'MOTHER, ANY DISTANCE . . .'

Mother, any distance greater than a single span
requires a second pair of hands.
You come to help me measure windows, pelmets,
     doors,
the acres of the walls, the prairies of the floors.

You at the zero-end, me with the spool of tape,
     recording
length, reporting metres, centimetres back to base,
     then leaving
up the stairs, the line still feeding out, unreeling
years between us. Anchor. Kite.

I space-walk through the empty bedrooms, climb
the ladder to the loft, to breaking point, where some-
                     thing
has to give;
two floors below your fingertips still pinch
the last one-hundredth of an inch . . . I reach
towards a hatch that opens on an endless sky
to fall or fly.

A BALLAD OF HOME

How we kissed
In our half-built house!
It was slightly timbered,
A bit bricked, on stilts,

We were newly married.
We drove out at dusk
And picked our way to safety
Through flints and grit and brick.

Like water through a porthole,
The sky poured in.
We sat on one step
Making estimations

And hugged until the watchman
Called and cursed and swung
His waterproof torch
Into our calculations.

Ten years on:
You wouldn't find now
An inch of spare ground.
Children in their cots,

Books, a cat, plants
Strain the walls' patience
And the last ounce of space.
And still every night

It all seems so sound.
But love why wouldn't it?
This house is built on our embrace
And there are worse foundations.

HOME, SWEET
HOME

The singing Kettle & the purring Cat,
The gentle Breathing of the cradled Babe . . .

S. T. COLERIDGE

Cling to thy home! If there the meanest shed
Yield thee a hearth and shelter for thy head,
And some poor plot with vegetables stor'd
Be all that Heaven allots thee for a board,
Unsavoury bread, and herbs that scatter'd grow
Wild on the river-brink or mountain-brow, –
Yet e'en this cheerless mansion shall provide
More heart's repose than all the world beside.

LEONIDAS OF ALEXANDIA (*fl.* 1st century CE)
TR. ROBERT BLAND

HOME HAPPINESS

Like a thing of the desert, alone in its glee,
I make a small home seem an empire to me;
Like a bird in the forest, whose world is its nest,
My home is my all, and the centre of rest.
Let Ambition stretch over the world at a stride,
Let the restless go rolling away with the tide,
I look on life's pleasures as follies at best,
And, like sunset, feel calm when I'm going to rest.

I sit by the fire, in the dark winter's night,
While the cat cleans her face with her foot in delight,
And the winds all a-cold, with rude clatter and din
Shake the windows, like robbers who want to come in;
Or else, from the cold to be hid and away,
By the bright burning fire see my children at play,
Making houses of cards, or a coach of a chair,
While I sit enjoying their happiness there.

I walk round the orchard on sweet summer eves,
And rub the perfume from the black-currant leaves,
Which, like the geranium, when touched, leave a smell
That lad's-love and sweet-briar can hardly excel.
I watch the plants grow, all begemmed with the
      shower,
That glitters like pearls in a sun-shiny hour;
And hear the pert robin just whistle a tune,
To cheer the lone hedger when labour is done.

Joys come like the grass in the fields springing there,
Without the mere toil of attention or care;
They come of themselves, like a star in the sky,
And the brighter they shine when the cloud passes by.
I wish but for little, and find it all there,
Where peace gives its faith to the home of the hare,
Who would else, overcome by her fears, run away
From the shade of the flower and the breeze of the day.

O the out-of-door blessings of leisure for me!
Health, riches, and joy! – it includes them all three.
There Peace comes to me – I have faith in her smile –
She's my playmate in leisure, my comfort in toil;
There the short pasture-grass hides the lark on its nest,
Though scarcely so high as the grasshopper's breast;
And there its moss-ball hides the wild honey-bee,
And there joy in plenty grows riches for me.

Far away from the world, its delusions and snares –
Whose words are but breath, and its breathing but
        cares, –
Where trouble's sown thick as the dews of the morn,
One can scarce set a foot without meeting a thorn –
There are some view the world as a lightly thrown
        ball,
There are some look on cities like stones in a wall –
Nothing more. There are others, Ambition's proud
        heirs,
Of whom I have neither the courage nor cares.

So I sit on my bench, or enjoy in the shade
My toil as a pasture, while using the spade;
My fancy is free in her pleasure to stray,
Making voyages round the whole world in a day.
I gather home-comforts where cares never grew,
Like manna, the heavens rain down with the dew,
Till I see the tired hedger bend wearily by,
Then like a tired bird to my corner I fly.

THE WINDOWS

How do you earn a life going on
behind yellow windows, writing at night
the Latin names of plants for a garden,
opening the front door to a wet dog?

Those you love forgive you, clearly,
with steaming casseroles and red wine.
It's the same film down all the suburban streets,
It's A Wonderful Life. How do you learn it?

What you hear – the doorbell's familiar chime.
What you touch – the clean, warm towels.
What you see what you smell what you taste
all tangible to the stranger passing your gate.

There you are again, in a room where those early
        hyacinths
surely sweeten the air, and the right words wait
in the dictionaries, on the tip of the tongue you touch
in a kiss, drawing your crimson curtains now

against dark hours. And again, in a kitchen,
the window ajar, sometimes the sound of your radio
or the scent of your food, and a cat in your arms,
a child in your arms, a lover. Such vivid flowers.

From A WINTER-EVENING HYMN
TO MY FIRE

What warm protection dost thou bend
Round curtained talk of friend with friend,
While the gray snow-storm, held aloof,
To softest outline rounds the roof,
Or the rude North with baffled strain
Shoulders the frost-starred window-pane!
Now the kind nymph to Bacchus born
By Morpheus' daughter, she that seems
Gifted upon her natal morn
By him with fire, by her with dreams,
Nicotia, dearer to the Muse
Than all the grapes' bewildering juice,
We worship, unforbid of thee;
And, as her incense floats and curls
In airy spires and wayward whirls,
Or poises on its tremulous stalk
A flower of frailest revery,
So winds and loiters, idly free,
The current of unguided talk,
Now laughter-rippled, and now caught
In smooth, dark pools of deeper thought.
Meanwhile thou mellowest every word,
A sweetly unobtrusive third;
For thou hast magic beyond wine,
To unlock natures each to each;
The unspoken thought thou canst divine:

Thou fill'st the pauses of the speech
With whispers that to dream-land reach
And frozen fancy-springs unchain
In Arctic outskirts of the brain:
Sun of all inmost confidences,
To thy rays doth the heart unclose
Its formal calyx of pretences,
That close against rude day's offences,
And open its shy midnight rose!

JAMES RUSSELL LOWELL (1819–91)

THE TREASURED THREE

Here with my treasured Three I sit,
    Here in my little house of joy,
Sharing one fire, and on one mat:
    My wife and my dog, Beauty Boy,
And my black Venus of a cat.

But while they sleep I sit and think;
    Will Death take my black Venus first;
Shall I be first, or Beauty Boy,
    Or Dinah, whom I love the most –
To leave this little house of joy?

A THANKSGIVING TO GOD
FOR HIS HOUSE

Lord, Thou hast given me a cell
        Wherein to dwell;
A little house, whose humble roof
        Is weatherproof,
Under the spars of which I lie
        Both soft and dry;
Where Thou, my chamber for to ward,
        Hast set a guard
Of harmless thoughts, to watch and keep
        Me while I sleep.
Low is my porch, as is my fate,
        Both void of state:
And yet the threshold of my door
        Is worn by th' poor,
Who thither come and freely get
        Good words or meat.
Like as my parlour, so my hall
        And kitchen's small:
A little buttery, and therein
        A little bin,
Which keeps my little loaf of bread
        Unchipped, unflead;
Some brittle sticks of thorn or briar
        Make me a fire,
Close by whose living coal I sit,
        And glow like it.

Lord, I confess too, when I dine,
            The pulse is Thine,
And all those other bits that be
            There placed by Thee;
The worts, the purslane, and the mess
            Of water-cress,
Which of Thy kindness Thou hast sent;
            And my content
Makes those, and my belovèd beet,
            To be more sweet.
'Tis Thou that crown'st my glittering hearth
            With guiltless mirth,
And giv'st me wassail bowls to drink,
            Spiced to the brink.
Lord, 'tis Thy plenty-dropping hand
            That soils my land,
And giv'st me, for my bushel sown,
            Twice ten for one:
Thou mak'st my teeming hen to lay
            Her egg each day;
Besides my healthful ewes to bear
            Me twins each year;
The while the conduits of my kine
            Run cream, for wine.
All these, and better Thou dost send
            Me, to this end,
That I should render, for my part,
            A thankful heart,

Which, fired with incense, I resign,
          As wholly Thine;
But the acceptance, that must be,
          My Christ, by Thee.

ROBERT HERRICK (1591 – 1674)

'I LEARNED – AT LEAST – WHAT HOME COULD BE –'

I learned – at least – what Home could be –
How ignorant I had been
Of pretty ways of Covenant –
How awkward at the Hymn

Round our new Fireside – but for this –
This pattern – of the Way –
Whose Memory drowns me, like the Dip
Of a Celestial Sea –

What Mornings in our Garden – guessed –
What Bees – for us – to hum –
With only Birds to interrupt
The Ripple of our Theme –

And Task for Both –
When Play be done –
Your Problem – of the Brain –
And mine – some foolisher effect –
A Ruffle – or a Tune –

The Afternoons – Together spent –
And Twilight – in the Lanes –
Some ministry to poorer lives –
Seen poorest – thro' our gains –

And then Return – and Night – and Home –

And then away to You to pass –
A new – diviner – care –
Till Sunrise take us back to Scene –
Transmuted – Vivider –

This seems a Home –
And Home is not –
But what that Place could be –
Afflicts me – as a Setting Sun –
Where Dawn – knows how to be –

From HOME AT GRASMERE

From that time forward was the place to me
As beautiful in thought as it had been
When present to my bodily eyes: a haunt
Of my affections, oftentimes in joy
A brighter joy, in sorrow (but of that
I have known little), in such gloom, at least,
Such damp of the gay mind as stood to me
In place of sorrow, 'twas a gleam of light –
And now 'tis mine for life! Dear vale,
One of thy lowly dwellings is my home.

. . .

Embrace me then, ye hills, and close me in;
Now in the clear and open day I feel
Your guardianship, I take it to my heart –
'Tis like the solemn shelter of the night.
But I would call thee beautiful, for mild
And soft and gay and beautiful thou art,
Dear valley, having in thy face a smile,
Though peaceful, full of gladness. Thou art pleased,
Pleased with thy crags and woody steeps, thy lake,
Its one green island and its winding shores,
The multitude of little rocky hills,
Thy church and cottages of mountain stone –
Clustered like stars, some few, but single most,
And lurking dimly in their shy retreats,
Or glancing at each other chearful looks,

Like separated stars with clouds between.
What want we? Have we not perpetual streams,
Warm woods and sunny hills, and fresh green fields,
And mountains not less green, and flocks and herds,
And thickets full of songsters, and the voice
Of lordly birds – an unexpected sound
Heard now and then from morn to latest eve
Admonishing the man who walks below
Of solitude and silence in the sky?
These have we, and a thousand nooks of earth
Have also these; but nowhere else is found –
Nowhere (or is it fancy?) can be found –
The one sensation that is here; 'tis here,
Here as it found its way into my heart
In childhood, here as it abides by day,
By night, here only; or in chosen minds
That take it with them hence, where'er they go.
'Tis (but I cannot name it), 'tis the sense
Of majesty and beauty and repose,
A blended holiness of earth and sky,
Something that makes this individual spot,
This small abiding-place of many men,
A termination and a last retreat,
A centre, come from whereso'er you will,
A whole without dependence or defect,
Made for itself and happy in itself,
Perfect contentment, unity entire.

A SENSE OF PLACE

If things had happened differently,
Maine or upper Michigan
might have given me a sense of place –

a topic that now consumes 87%
of all commentary on American literature.

I might have run naked by a bayou
or been beaten near a shrouded cove on a coastline.

Arizona could have raised me.
Even New York's Westchester County
with its stone walls scurrying up into the woods
could have been the spot to drop a couple of roots.

But as it is, the only thing that gives me
a sense of place is this upholstered chair
with its dark brown covers,
angled into a room near a corner window.

I am the native son of only this wingback seat
standing dutifully on four squat legs,
its two arms open in welcome,

illuminated by a swan-neck lamp
and accompanied by a dog-like hassock,
the closest thing a chair has to a pet.

This is my landscape –
a tobacco-colored room,

the ceiling with its river-like crack,
the pond of a mirror on one wall
a pen and ink drawing of a snarling fish on another.

And behind me a long porch
from which the sky may be viewed,
sometimes stippled with high clouds,
and crossed now and then by a passing bird –
little courier with someplace to go –

other days crowded with thunderheads,
the light turning an alarming green,
the air stirred by the nostrils of apocalyptic horses,
and me slumped in my chair, my back to it all.

BILLY COLLINS (1941 –)

HOME IS SO SAD

Home is so sad. It stays as it was left,
Shaped to the comfort of the last to go
As if to win them back. Instead, bereft
Of anyone to please, it withers so,
Having no heart to put aside the theft

And turn again to what it started as,
A joyous shot at how things ought to be,
Long fallen wide. You can see how it was:
Look at the pictures and the cutlery.
The music in the piano stool. That vase.

PHILIP LARKIN (1922–85)

DAY 60

I used to think I was an early riser,
but she's here when I wake up
staring me in the face like I can't see her.

She leans on my shoulder when I'm writing,
imitates me on the phone, follows me

into the sitting-room, lies on the sofa
as if she belongs here, and she thinks
it's alright to interrupt my reading.

I leave her at home when I go to the beach.

She doesn't know how silver sand curves
beside the sea for miles, reflecting blues,
how no one else is here, and I can stand

at the edge of the waves in the wind
breathing out to indigo on the horizon.

As soon as I get back, she's beside me,
when I take off my boots, when I hang up
my coat, when I wash my hands at the sink.

She opens the white wine well before six,
and makes me stay up until after midnight,
which I would never normally do.

No one seems to know how long
she will be staying, and I'm afraid to ask.

The wet windy grey days are the worst.

PAULINE PRIOR-PITT (1940–)

PROSPECT HEIGHTS LAMENT

On the first day I took secateurs to Prospect Park
    and cut out some forsythia.
On the second day I ate garlic by the bulb.
On the third day I heard the crackle of my lungs and
    remembered hiding out once in an attic padded
    with fiberglass.
On the fourth day I watched the neighbors leave.
On the fifth day I ordered pineapple linzer sandwich
    cookies from the shut-down tea-house.
On the sixth day, countryhouseless, I thought
    of Basho:
In Kyoto,
hearing the cuckoo,
I long for Kyoto.
From black bananas I made bread.
Then I gambled in the stock market with the extra
    black bananas.
Then my Adam's apple became a sweet gumball fruit.
    Then an avocado stone.
Then I stood on my balcony and cried for the clerks
    and the nurses.
I cried for my city wheezing under its viral load.
I cried for the ventilators lost in the warehouses.
Then I ordered a nebulizer, Sunshine chorella tablets,
    meyer lemons, 91% isopropyl rubbing alcohol,
    albuterol, Annie's Shells and Cheese, and
    macadamia nut milk over the internet.

Then I attended a funeral on Zoom.
Then I learned how to be a crow and a pigeon.
Then I sweat out what had entered via my thumb pad
    into the corner of my eye.
Then I gave up my unclean hands to the sky and got
    on my clothesline and sang for the dead.

STAY HOME

I will wait here in the fields
to see how well the rain
brings on the grass.
In the labor of the fields
longer than a man's life
I am home. Don't come with me.
You stay home too.

I will be standing in the woods
where the old trees
move only with the wind
and then with gravity.
In the stillness of the trees
I am at home. Don't come with me.
You stay home too.

REMOVALS

But ah, how difficult it is to go! We flatter ourselves with fancied freedom. We are the slaves of every house that belongs to us. Invisible chains bind us to every chair and table.

MARY E. COLERIDGE

Go to your wide futures, you said.

GRACE NICHOLS

TO A DAUGHTER LEAVING HOME

When I taught you
at eight to ride
a bicycle, loping along
beside you
as you wobbled away
on two round wheels,
my own mouth rounding
in surprise when you pulled
ahead down the curved
path of the park,
I kept waiting
for the thud
of your crash as I
sprinted to catch up,
while you grew
smaller, more breakable
with distance,
pumping, pumping
for your life, screaming
with laughter,
the hair flapping
behind you like a
handkerchief waving
goodbye.

LOT'S WIFE

The just man followed then his angel guide
Where he strode on the black highway, hulking
    and bright;
But a wild grief in his wife's bosom cried,
Look back, it is not too late for a last sight

Of the red towers of your native Sodom, the square
Where once you sang, the gardens you shall mourn,
And the tall house with empty windows where
You loved your husband and your babes were born.

She turned, and looking on the bitter view
Her eyes were welded shut by mortal pain;
Into transparent salt her body grew,
And her quick feet were rooted in the plain.

Who would waste tears upon her? Is she not
The least of our losses, this unhappy wife?
Yet in my heart she will not be forgot
Who, for a single glance, gave up her life.

ANNA AKHMATOVA (1889–1966)
48   TR. RICHARD WILBUR

TRISTIA

All there is to know on the art of leaving
I've learned in careful pillow-talk at night.
The oxen ruminate. It'll soon be morning;
The night watch does its rounds, round to the light.
I trace the rubric of the cockerel darkness
When, taking up his road, with brimming eyes,
The one who's leaving suddenly feels its harshness
Hit home: the muses' song, the women's cries.
Who can tell what an abstract noun like 'leaving'
Will come to mean, when it's our turn?
What are we to make of the cockerel crowing
When midnight flames in the citadel still burn?
And in the dawn of some new life or other
With oxen ruminating in the hay,
Why does the herald of this new world order
Preen on the battlements to greet the day?
I love the ordinariness of fabric:
The shuttle, warp and weft, the spindle's hum.
And here she's: barefoot, feather-light, in cambric
Shift, running to meet you, glad you've come.
Our life is threadbare, and the words to measure
Joy are worn thin with repetition;
We'll keep on using them, but what we treasure
Now is just the flash of recognition.
So be it, then. A translucent figure
Lies on a clean, clay dish; a squirrel's pelt
Stretched out. A girl, a fortune-teller

Waits to see which way the wax will melt.
It's not for us to test the reaper's mettle;
The wax is lost on women, bronze on men.
For us the die is only cast in battle;
Vision is theirs, at the living end.

OSIP MANDELSTAM (1891 – 1938)
TR. PETER McCAREY

EXIT

Just when hope withers, a reprieve is granted.
The door opens onto a street like in the movies,
clean of people, of cats; except it is *your* street
you are leaving. Reprieve has been granted,
'provisionally' – a fretful word.

The windows you have closed behind
you are turning pink, doing what they do
every dawn. Here it's gray; the door
to the taxicab waits. This suitcase,
the saddest object in the world.

Well, the world's open. And now through
the windshield the sky begins to blush,
as you did when your mother told you
what it took to be a woman in this life.

50   RITA DOVE (1952-)

HOW ARE THE CHILDREN ROBIN
For Robin Skelton

It does not matter how are you how are
The children flying leaving home so early?
The song is lost asleep the blackthorn breaks
Into its white flourish. The poet walks
At all odd times hoping the road is empty.
I mean me walking hoping the road is empty.

Not that I would ever expect to see
Them over the brow of the hill coming
In scarlet anoraks to meet their Dad.
A left, a right, my mad feet trudge the road
Between the busy times. It raineth now
Across the hedges and beneath the bough.

It does not matter let that be a lesson
To cross the fields. Keep off the road. The Black
Wood of Madron with its roof of rooks
Is lost asleep flying into the dusk.
When shall we see the children older returning
Into the treetops? And what are they bringing?

W. S. GRAHAM (1918–86)

A REMOVAL FROM TERRY STREET

On a squeaking cart, they push the usual stuff,
A mattress, bed ends, cups, carpets, chairs,
Four paperback westerns. Two whistling youths
In surplus U.S. Army battle-jackets
Remove their sister's goods. Her husband
Follows, carrying on his shoulders the son
Whose mischief we are glad to see removed,
And pushing, of all things, a lawnmower.
There is no grass in Terry Street. The worms
Come up cracks in concrete yards in moonlight.
That man, I wish him well. I wish him grass.

REFLECTIONS ON HAVING LEFT A PLACE OF RETIREMENT

Sermoni propriora. - Hor.

Low was our pretty Cot: our tallest Rose
Peep'd at the chamber-window. We could hear
At silent noon, and eve, and early morn,
The Sea's faint murmur. In the open air
Our Myrtles blossom'd; and across the porch
Thick Jasmins twined: the little landscape round
Was green and woody, and refresh'd the eye.
It was a spot which you might aptly call
The Valley of Seclusion! Once I saw
(Hallowing his Sabbath-day by quietness)
A wealthy son of Commerce saunter by,
Bristowa's citizen: methought, it calm'd
His thirst of idle gold, and made him muse
With wiser feelings: for he paus'd, and look'd
With a pleas'd sadness, and gaz'd all around,
Then eyed our Cottage, and gaz'd round again,
And sigh'd, and said, it was a Blesséd Place.
And we *were* bless'd. Oft with patient ear
Long-listening to the viewless sky-lark's note
(Viewless, or haply for a moment seen
Gleaming on sunny wings) in whisper'd tones
I've said to my Belovéd, 'Such, sweet Girl!
The inobtrusive song of Happiness,
Unearthly minstrelsy! then only heard

When the Soul seeks to hear; when all is hush'd,
And the Heart listens!'
                But the time, when first
From that low Dell, steep up the stony Mount
I climb'd with perilous toil and reach'd the top,
Oh! what a goodly scene! *Here* the bleak mount,
The bare bleak mountain speckled thin with sheep;
Grey clouds, that shadowing spot the sunny fields;
And river, now with bushy rocks o'er-brow'd,
Now winding bright and full, with naked banks;
And seats, and lawns, the Abbey and the wood,
And cots, and hamlets, and faint city-spire;
The Channel *there*, the Islands and white sails,
Dim coasts, and cloud-like hills, and shoreless Ocean –
It seem'd like Omnipresence! God, methought,
Had built him there a Temple: the whole World
Seem'd *imag'd* in its vast circumference:
No *wish* profan'd my overwhelméd heart.
Blest hour! It was a luxury, – to be!

Ah! quiet Dell! dear Cot, and Mount sublime!
I was constrain'd to quit you. Was it right,
While my unnumber'd brethren toil'd and bled,
That I should dream away the entrusted hours
On rose-leaf beds, pampering the coward heart
With feelings all too delicate for use?
Sweet is the tear that from some Howard's eye
Drops on the cheek of one he lifts from earth:
And he that works me good with unmov'd face,

Does it but half: he chills me while he aids,
My benefactor, not my brother man!
Yet even this, this cold beneficence
Praise, praise it, O my Soul! oft as thou scann'st
The sluggard Pity's vision-weaving tribe!
Who sigh for Wretchedness, yet shun the Wretched,
Nursing in some delicious solitude
Their slothful loves and dainty sympathies!
I therefore go, and join head, heart, and hand,
Active and firm, to fight the bloodless fight
Of Science, Freedom, and the Truth in Christ.

Yet oft when after honourable toil
Rests the tir'd mind, and waking loves to dream,
My spirit shall revisit thee, dear Cot!
Thy Jasmin and thy window-peeping Rose,
And Myrtles fearless of the mild sea-air.
And I shall sigh fond wishes – sweet Abode!
Ah! – had none greater! And that all had such!
It might be so – but the time is not yet.
Speed it, O Father! Let thy Kingdom come!

LOVING A HOUSE

Sandi doesn't like Dan much, but loves his house. She comes over before he's home from work, to gaze into its window-eyes.

She wheedles her own key. ('That's good,' Dan thinks. 'We're getting close.') Now she can visit when he isn't there to interrupt as her bare feet caress the hardwood floors, as her hands linger on gleaming knobs and faucets, as she strokes the long, smooth balustrade, and explores every chamber of this heart she adores.

Though Dan's frog-belly makes her wince, his slobbery kiss makes her shudder, the feel of him inside her can only be endured if she is drunk or stoned, she marries him, pretending it's the house on top of her, the house into whose ear she cries, to whom she whispers, 'I love you. Good night.'

How awful when, after a year of bliss, Dan wins promotion to a better town.

The 'For Sale' sign in the yard pierces her heart.

She makes phone calls. She hires workmen and machines. Dan comes home with two First Class tickets, to find wife and house gone.

'We'll move from state to state,' she mouths through the rear window of the truck that tows her love. 'We'll paint, remodel, whatever it takes.'

When rain begins to fall, she climbs from the truck to the house, and as asphalt hisses by, kisses the wet windows one by one. 'It's hard for me, too, Sweetheart,' she whispers. 'Please don't cry.'

Somehow I really want to go
To Leningrad

I really want to go to Leningrad

Only I really want to go

To Leningrad

And back

VSEVOLOD NEKRASOV (1934–2009)
TR. GERALD JANECEK

THE TRUTH OF DEPARTURE

With each journey it gets
worse
what kind of learning is that
when that is what we are born for

and harder and harder to find
what is hanging on
to what
all day it has been raining
and I have been writing letters
the pearl curtains

stroking the headlands
under immense dark clouds
the valley sighing with rain
everyone home and quiet

what will become of all these
things that I see
that are here and are me
and I am none of them
what will become
of the bench and the teapot
the pencils and the kerosene lamps
all the books all the writing
the green of the leaves
what becomes of the house
and the island
and the sound of your footstep

who knows it is here
who says it will stay
who says I will know it
who said it would be all right

EAST, WEST,
HOME'S BEST

... perhaps the self-same song that found a path
Through the sad heart of Ruth, when sick for home,
She stood in tears amid the alien corn.

JOHN KEATS

Stands the Church clock at ten to three?
And is there honey still for tea?

RUPERT BROOKE

Stay, stay at home, my heart, and rest;
Home-keeping hearts are happiest,
For those that wander they know not where
Are full of trouble and full of care;
    To stay at home is best.

Weary and homesick and distressed,
They wander east, they wander west,
And are baffled and beaten and blown about
By the winds of the wilderness of doubt;
    To stay at home is best.

Then stay at home, my heart, and rest;
The bird is safest in its nest;
O'er all that flutter their wings and fly
A hawk is hovering in the sky;
    To stay at home is best.

HENRY WADSWORTH LONGFELLOW (1807–82)

HOME-THOUGHTS, FROM ABROAD

Oh, to be in England
Now that April's there,
And whoever wakes in England
Sees, some morning, unaware,
That the lowest boughs and the brushwood sheaf
Round the elm-tree bole are in tiny leaf,
While the chaffinch sings on the orchard bough
In England – now!

And after April, when May follows,
And the whitethroat builds, and all the swallows!
Hark, where my blossomed pear-tree in the hedge
Leans to the field and scatters on the clover
Blossoms and dewdrops – at the bent spray's edge –
That's the wise thrush; he sings each song twice over,
Lest you should think he never could recapture
The first fine careless rapture!
And though the fields look rough with hoary dew,
All will be gay when noontide wakes anew
The buttercups, the little children's dower
– Far brighter than this gaudy melon-flower!

CONSOLATION

How agreeable it is not to be touring Italy this summer,
wandering its cities and ascending its torrid
    hilltowns.
How much better to cruise these local, native streets,
fully comprehending every roadsign and billboard
and all the sudden hand gestures of my compatriots.

There are no abbeys here, no pale frescoes or famous
domes and no one is expected to know a succession
of despots or tour the corners of a torture chamber.
There is no need to touch a sarcophagus,
    see Napoleon's
bed on Elba or view the bones of a saint under glass.

How much better to command the modest precinct
    of home
than to be dwarfed by pillar, arch and basilica.
Why bury my head in phrasebooks and maps?
Why feed scenery to a hungry one-eyed camera
eager to eat the world one monument at a time?

Instead of slouching in a cafe ignorant of the word
    for ice,
I will head down to the coffee shop and the waitress
known as Dot. I will slide into the flow of the morning
paper, all language barriers down,
rivers of idiom running freely, eggs over easy on
    the way.

And after breakfast I will not have to find someone
to take my picture with the owner and his wife.
I will not puzzle over the bill or record in a journal
everything I had to eat, how the sun came in
      the window.
It is enough to climb back into the car

as if it were the great car of English itself
and sounding my loud vernacular horn, drive off down
a road that will never lead to Rome, not even Bologna.

BILLY COLLINS (1941–)

From THE REGRETS

Happy the Ulysses who gets back home,
The Jason who conquers the golden fleece,
They can be full of reason and experience
And impress the relatives who did not go!
But when shall I see my little village,
With its smoking chimneys, at what time of year
Shall I see my not magnificent house which is more
To me than a province, though that may sound silly?
The little place built by my ancestors
Pleases me more than Roman palaces,
And all this marble is nothing to my slate:
I prefer my Loire to the Latin Tiber
And my little Liré to the Palatine,
And the soft air of Anjou to this climate.

JOACHIM DU BELLAY (c. 1522–60)
TR. C. H. SISSON

From TRISTIA (III, 12)

The wind is out of the west again to inspire the frozen
   Pontus and bring the rigid corpse of the land
to life again. The bleak fields of brown stubble
   show a little green in the fresh shoots.
The slate gray of the sky relents to a shade not far
   from a real blue. There's a hint behind the morning
haze of a sun that may yet burn through a fair day
   when boys and girls will run through meadows to
       gather
wildflowers, and birds will chatter or even sing
   as anywhere else in the world. Somewhere, I guess
vines are coming to bud. (There are no vines around here.)
   Somewhere trees are sprouting those tiny leaves.
(There are no trees around here.) But the air is a little
       milder;
   one can breathe without feeling the daggers
of cold attacking one's breast, or even think of home
   where the festivals are impending with chariot races
and mock battles. The athletes are working out or
       soaking
   sore muscles . . . The theaters are all busy
with the new season's productions. The city's pulse
       quickens
   and its citizens feel their own quickening with it,
those happy souls who take its rich arrondissements
   for granted, as I did, myself, once.
Now, I look about me, watching the snow turn
   to mud, watching the ice melt beneath

a grudging sun. The grip of winter shows some sign
   of relaxing again. Ships will appear in the harbor,
and I shall go running down with the others to ask
         whence
      they've come, and what they carry, and whither
         bound,
and what is their home port. The answer is almost
         always
   a disappointment, the name of another savage
anchorage up or down this same barbarous coast.
   Only the rare captain has taken his craft
across the distant seas from the parts of the world
         where Greek
   or – even better – Latin sings in the air
with the ease of the wind's wordless wailing through
         the shrouds
      above the wordless menace of the crew
whom the angry gulls scold, fly off, and then wheel back
   to scold again. Sometimes a skipper or mate
with a civil tongue in his head can, for a glass of wine,
      retail the news or rumors he's picked up
from a fortunate wind beyond the straits of the
         Hellespont.
   I sit in the tavern with such fellows and hope
for word of some good fortune for Caesar that might
         occasion
   a triumph, rejoicing, or even some general pardon.
Have the Germans yielded at last, recognizing the
         power
      to which they must bow their stiff necks or die?

Has Tiberius taught them the lesson any fool should
    have learned
  from Julius Caesar? The man who brings me report
of such good news I shall drag at once to my table to
    serve
  the best feast Tomis can offer. My home
shall be his to command. Or say, my residence, rather,
  for Naso is not at home here. Scythia's only
a temporary abode – or else a burial plot,
  if the gods do not prompt Caesar to relent.

OVID (43 BCE–17 CE)
TR. DAVID R. SLAVITT

REMEMBERING SILVES

Well, Abū Bakr,
greet my home place in Silves
and ask the people there
if, as I think, they still remember me.

Greet the Palace of the Balconies
on behalf of a young man
still nostalgic for that place.

Warriors like lions lived there
and white gazelles
in what beautiful forests
and in what beautiful lairs!

How many pleasurable nights I spent
in the shadow of the palace
with women of opulent hips
and delicate waists:

blonds and brunettes.
My soul remembers them
as shining swords and dark lances.

With one girl I spent
many delicious nights
beside the bend of the river.
Her bracelet resembled
the curve of the current

and as the hours went by
she offered me the wine
of her glance or that of her glass
and sometimes that of her lips.

The strings of her lute
wounded by the plectrum
caused me to shiver
as if I had heard a melody
played by swords on the
neck tendons of the enemy.

When she took off her cloak
and revealed her waist,
a flowering willow branch,
it was like a bud
opening to reveal the flower.

KING AL-MU'TAMID OF SEVILLA (1040–95)
TR. COLA FRANZEN

I BELONG THERE

I belong there. I have many memories. I was born as
     everyone is born.
I have a mother, a house with many windows,
     brothers, friends, and a prison cell
with a chilly window! I have a wave snatched by
     seagulls, a panorama of my own.
I have a saturated meadow. In the deep horizon of my
     word, I have a moon,
a bird's sustenance, and an immortal olive tree.
I have lived on the land long before swords turned
     man into prey.
I belong there. When heaven mourns for her mother,
     I return heaven to her mother.
And I cry so that a returning cloud might carry my
     tears.
To break the rules, I have learned all the words
     needed for a trial by blood.
I have learned and dismantled all the words in order
     to draw from them a single word: *Home.*

MAHMOUD DARWISH (1941–2008)
68   TR. MUNIR AKASH AND CAROLYN FORCHÉ

OF THE WARRES IN IRELAND

I prais'd the speech, but cannot now abide it,
That warre is sweet to those that have not try'd it,
For I have prov'd it now, and plainly see't
It is so sweet, it maketh all things sweet.
At home, Canarie wine and Greek grow lothsome:
Here milk is nectar; water tasteth toothsome.
There without baked, rost, boyl'd, it has no cheere:
Bisket we like, and Bonny Clabo here.
There we complaine of one rare roasted chick:
Here viler meat worse cook't ne're makes me sick.
At home in silken sparvers, beds of downe
We scant can rest, but still tosse up and downe:
Here we can sleep, a saddle to our pillow,
A hedge the curtaine, canopy a willow,
There if a child but cry, O what a spite!
Here we can brook three 'larms in one night.
There homely rooms must be perfum'd with roses:
Here match and powder ne're offende our noses:
There from a storme of raine we run like pullets:
Here we stand fast against a showre of bullets.
Lo then, how greatly their opinions erre,
That think there is no great delight in warre.
  But yet for this (sweet warre) Ile be thy debtor,
  I shall for ever love my home the better.

SIR JOHN HARINGTON (1561–1612)   69

HOME NEWS

'My dear son I am well thanks be to God
I pray for you day and night.'

'My dear brother it's my sad duty to announce
the death of our beloved mother
Which occurred last Sunday
after a short illness.'

'My cousin I've grown a lot
send me some trousers and new shoes.'

'My love, it's now ten years I've been awaiting you
What's keeping you there in the white man's land
think of the trouble you cause us
by such a long absence.'

'My dear friend our country's changing
into a huge shanty-town.
No one can eat his fill except . . .
Send me a tape-recorder.'

'My dear son it is I your father
I beg you to return to your land
if not you will not have even
the sorrow of recognizing my tomb.'

'My dear nephew, I must tell you
of your father's death
we all hope you'll be able to attend
the forty-days' wake.'

'My dear . . .'
A tear yesterday when the postman passed
Anxiety today in awaiting his return
The abyss of sadness envelops me
When I have no news from home.
My soul shrivels a little
When home news tumbles over me.
The other day I made a fleeting boat
Full of home news.
I set it in the water at the wharf of Exile-Overseas.
I went to attend its arrival
at the landing stage of Loneliness-under-Hope.
My boat landed some secret passengers for me
Next day the postman's prophetic hand was
stretched towards me.

'My dear friend, your brother was arrested
last week in reprisal
for your political work against the government
Your family is left without a head
Send me a shirt and a neck-tie.'

AHMED TIDJANI-CISSÉ (1941–2015)
TR. GERALD MOORE

HOMESICKNESS

Homesickness! Long ago revealed
as fraudulent delusion.
I don't care where
I am alone. It doesn't matter

across what streets, into what house
I drag myself, and my shopping basket –
a house that doesn't know I'm there,
like a hospital or barracks.

I don't care who sees me lie
like a caged lion, snarling slowly,
nor from what society they
thrust me, force me out into

my own internal solitude,
a polar bear in tropic water.
I don't care where I am hurt,
nor where I am insulted.

I do not love my native tongue,
its weak, breast-fed attraction.
I am indifferent to the words
in which someone misunderstands me

(someone who reads magazines
and thrives on gossip columns).
He is Twentieth-Century Man –
my own age was never numbered.

Struck dumb, a rotting log
that marked a path now forgotten.
And I don't care. All things are strange.
All facts. And perhaps what once

was closest is strangest of all.
All signs upon me, all traces
and dates seem wiped away.
A soul. Born. Somewhere. Or other.

My homeland cared so little for me
any clever sleuth
may search my soul –
he will find no birthmark.

Each house is strange, each altar bare.
And I don't care. It doesn't matter.
But if, beside the autumn road, I see
a rowan-tree . . .

MARINA TSVETAEVA (1892–1941)
TR. PAUL SCHMIDT

HOME

How brightly glistening in the sun
    The woodland ivy plays!
While yonder beeches from their barks
    Reflect his silver rays.

That sun surveys a lovely scene
    From softly smiling skies;
And wildly through unnumbered trees
    The wind of winter sighs:

Now loud, it thunders o'er my head,
    And now in distance dies.
But give me back my barren hills,
    Where colder breezes rise;

Where scarce the scattered, stunted trees
    Can yield an answering swell,
But where a wilderness of heath
    Returns the sound as well.

For yonder garden, fair and wide,
    With groves of evergreen,
Long winding walks, and borders trim,
    And velvet lawns between –

Restore to me that little spot,
    With grey walls compassed round,
Where knotted grass neglected lies,
    And weeds usurp the ground.

Though all around this mansion high
    Invites the foot to roam,
And though its halls are fair within –
    Oh, give me back my Home!

ANNE BRONTË (1820–49)

NIGHT THOUGHTS

In front of my bed the moonlight is very bright.
I wonder if that can be frost on the floor?
I lift up my head and look full at the full moon,
      the dazzling moon.
I drop my head and think of the home of old days.

LI T'AI-PO (701–62)
TR. AMY LOWELL

HOMESICK FOR THE EARTH

One day we'll say 'The sun ruled then.
Don't you remember how it shone on the twigs,
on the old, as well as the wide-eyed young?
It knew how to make all things vivid
the second it alighted on them.
It could run just like the racehorse.
How can we forget the time we had on earth?
If we dropped a plate it clattered.
We'd look around like connoisseurs,
alert to the slightest nuance of the air,
knew if a friend was coming towards us.
We'd pick daffodils, collect pebbles, shells –
when we couldn't catch the smoke.
Now smoke is all we hold in our hands.'

JULES SUPERVIELLE (1884–1960)
76   TR. MONIZA ALVI

HOMECOMINGS

'Home is the place where, when you have to go there,
They have to take you in.'
                    'I should have called it
Something you somehow haven't to deserve.'

ROBERT FROST

CARMEN XXXI

Of all peninsulas and islands
The inner and the outer Neptune
Bear upon lakes or the great sea
Sirmio is delectable. With what pleasure
I see it again, hardly believing that I have left
The plains of Thynia and Bythinia.
What is more pleasant than to dispense with trouble?
The mind puts down her load and, tired with travel,
We come to our Lares and rest in our own beds.
This is really all we undertake these toils for.
Elegant Sirmio, I salute you.
Be glad your master has come.
Be glad, waters of the Lydian lake.
Laugh, whatever laughter there is in the house.

CATULLUS (c. 84–c. 54 BCE)
TR. C. H. SISSON

TWO HUNDRED MILES

From the front of this house a road runs
and I am already gone.
Across the miles of moons and suns
I am running already.

Down the hill to the bridge,
over the bridge to the town,
through the town to the plain,
up the range and down.

O back to my red mountain
and along the red road,
and at the green gate
I put down my load.

All I want is to see you.
Nothing matters at all;
not the buds on the peach-tree,
or the new leaf on the fern,
or the hyacinth if it is flowering,
or the spring green on the hill.
I have come so far; why have I come?
Only because you are my home.

From THE ODYSSEY

'Strange woman! So hard – the gods of Olympus
made you harder than any other woman in the world!
What other wife could have a spirit so unbending?
Holding back from her husband, home at last for *her*
after bearing twenty years of brutal struggle.
Come, nurse, make me a bed. I'll sleep alone.
She has a heart of iron in her breast.'

                          'Strange *man*,'
wary Penelope said. 'I'm not so proud, so scornful,
nor am I overwhelmed by your quick change . . .
You look – how well I know – the way he looked,
setting sail from Ithaca years ago
aboard the long-oared ship.

                      Come, Eurycleia,
move the sturdy bedstead out of our bridal chamber –
that room the master built with his own hands.
Take it out now, sturdy bed that it is,
and spread it deep with fleece,
blankets and lustrous throws to keep him warm.'

Putting her husband to the proof – but Odysseus
blazed up in fury, lashing out at his loyal wife:
'Woman – your words, they cut me to the core!
Who could move my bed? Impossible task,
even for some skilled craftsman – unless a god
came down in person, quick to lend a hand,
lifted it out with ease and moved it elsewhere.
Not a man on earth, not even at peak strength,
would find it easy to prise it up and shift it, no,

a great sign, a hallmark lies in its construction.
I know, I built it myself – no one else . . .
There was a branching olive-tree inside our court,
grown to its full prime, the bole like a column,
    thickset.
Around it I built my bedroom, finished off the walls
with good tight stonework, roofed it over soundly
and added doors, hung well and snugly wedged.
Then I lopped the leafy crown of the olive,
clean-cutting the stump bare from roots up,
planing it round with a bronze smoothing-adze –
I had the skill – I shaped it plumb to the line to make
my bedpost, bored the holes it needed with an auger.
Working from there I built my bed, start to finish,
I gave it ivory inlays, gold and silver fittings,
wove the straps across it, oxhide gleaming red.
There's our secret sign, I tell you, our life story!
Does the bed, my lady, still stand planted firm? –
I don't know – or has someone chopped away
that olive-trunk and hauled our bedstead off?'
                      Living proof –
Penelope felt her knees go slack, her heart surrender,
recognizing the strong clear signs Odysseus offered.
She dissolved in tears, rushed to Odysseus, flung
    her arms
around his neck and kissed his head and cried out,
'*Odysseus* – don't flare up at me now, not you,
always the most understanding man alive!
The gods, it was the gods who sent us sorrow –
they grudged us both a life in each other's arms

from the heady zest of youth to the stoop of old age.
But don't fault me, angry with me now because I failed,
at the first glimpse, to greet you, hold you, so . . .
In my heart of hearts I always cringed with fear
some fraud might come, beguile me with his talk;
the world is full of the sort . . .
But now, since you have revealed such overwhelming
        proof —
the secret sign of our bed, which no one's ever seen
but you and I and a single handmaid, Actoris,
the servant my father gave me when I came,
who kept the doors of our room you built so well . . .
you've conquered my heart, my hard heart, at last!'

The more she spoke, the more a deep desire for tears
welled up inside his breast — he wept as he held the wife
he loved, the soul of loyalty, in his arms at last.
Joy, warm as the joy that shipwrecked sailors feel
when they catch sight of land — Poseidon has struck
their well-rigged ship on the open sea with gale winds
and crushing walls of waves, and only a few escape,
        swimming,
struggling out of the frothing surf to reach the shore,
their bodies crusted with salt but buoyed up with joy
as they plant their feet on solid ground again,
spared a deadly fate. So joyous now to her
the sight of her husband, vivid in her gaze,
that her white arms, embracing his neck
would never for a moment let him go . . .

HOMER (*fl.* 9th/8th century BCE)
TR. ROBERT FAGLES   83

WHO LOVES YOU

I worry about you travelling in those mystical
        machines.
Every day people fall from the clouds, dead.
Breathe in and out and in and out easy.
Safety, safely, safe home.

Your photograph is in the fridge, smiles when the
        light comes on.
All the time people are burnt in the public places.
Rest where the cool trees drop to a gentle shade.
Safety, safely, safe home.

Don't lie down on the sands where the hole in
        the sky is.
Too many people being gnawed to shreds.
Send me your voice however it comes across oceans.
Safety, safely, safe home.

The loveless men and homeless boys are out there
        and angry.
Nightly people end their lives in the shortcut.
Walk in the light, steadily hurry towards me.
Safety, safely, safe home. (Who loves you?)
Safety, safely, safe home.

COMING HOME

The bar is full of English cigarette smoke
and English voices, getting louder
– a language lumpy as a ploughed field.
It's hard to believe our tongues have got it too.

People are growing drunk at the thought of home.
The sea patiently knits its wide grey sleeve.
No one else comes up to lean on the rail
where, damp and silent, we watch

the long white skirts of land drifting
sadly through mist, as if a young girl sat
by the shore still, waiting for a bluebird.
It's September, and already winter.

And now the toy-sized train
is creeping with its worn-out battery
and a cargo of sandwiches and arguments
over grey-green fields into grey-white suburbs.

We're playing a game with the streets
– spreading them out and tying them up again;
when they've caught us, we're home.
The lawn blows like a tiny English Channel.

We chug towards our own front door
anxiously, seeing as if for the first time
how tight the plot that locks us in,
how small our parts, now unchosen.

CAROL RUMENS (1944–)   85

HOMECOMING

The present reigned supreme
　　Like the shallow floods over the gutters
Over the raw paths where we had been,
　　The house with the shutters.

Too strange the sudden change
　　Of the times we buried when we left
The times before we had properly arranged
　　The memories that we kept.

Our sapless roots have fed
　　The wind-swept seedlings of another age.
Luxuriant weeds have grown where we led
　　The Virgins to the water's edge.

There at the edge of the town
　　Just by the burial ground
Stands the house without a shadow
　　Lived in by new skeletons.

That is all that is left
　　To greet us on the home-coming
After we have paced the world
　　And longed for returning.

THE PRODIGAL SON

Here come I to my own again,
Fed, forgiven and known again,
Claimed by bone of my bone again
    And cheered by flesh of my flesh.
The fatted calf is dressed for me,
But the husks have greater zest for me,
I think my pigs will be best for me,
    So I'm off to the Yards afresh.

I never was very refined, you see,
(And it weighs on my brother's mind, you see)
But there's no reproach among swine, d'you see,
    For being a bit of a swine.
So I'm off with wallet and staff to eat
The bread that is three parts chaff to wheat,
But glory be! – there's a laugh to it,
    Which isn't the case when we dine.

My father glooms and advises me,
My brother sulks and despises me,
And Mother catechises me
    Till I want to go out and swear.
And, in spite of the butler's gravity,
I know that the servants have it I
Am a monster of moral depravity,
    And I'm damned if I think it's fair!

I wasted my substance, I know I did,
On riotous living, so I did,
But there's nothing on record to show I did
    Worse than my betters have done.
They talk of the money I spent out there –
They hint at the pace that I went out there –
But they all forget I was sent out there
    Alone as a rich man's son.

So I was a mark for plunder at once,
And lost my cash (can you wonder?) at once,
But I didn't give up and knock under at once,
    I worked in the Yards for a spell,
Where I spent my nights and my days with hogs.
And shared their milk and maize with hogs,
Till, I guess, I have learned what pays with hogs
    And – I have that knowledge to sell!

So back I go to my job again,
Not so easy to rob again,
Or quite so ready to sob again
    On any neck that's around.
I'm leaving, Pater. Good-bye to you!
God bless you, Mater! I'll write to you!
I wouldn't be impolite to you,
    But, Brother, you are a hound!

HOMECOMING

He was back. Said nothing.
But it was clear something unpleasant had occurred.
He lay down in his suit.
Hid his head under the blanket.
Drew up his knees.
He's about forty, but not at this moment.
He exists – but only as much as in his mother's belly
behind seven skins, in protective darkness.
Tomorrow he is lecturing on homeostasis
In metagalactic space-travel.
But now he's curled up and fallen asleep.

WISLAWA SZYMBORSKA (1923–2012)
TR. ADAM CZERNIAWSKI

AT HOME

When I was dead, my spirit turned
    To seek the much-frequented house:
I passed the door, and saw my friends
    Feasting beneath green orange boughs;
From hand to hand they pushed the wine,
    They sucked the pulp of plum and peach;
They sang, they jested, and they laughed,
    For each was loved of each.

I listened to their honest chat:
    Said one 'Tomorrow we shall be
Plod plod along the featureless sands,
    And coasting miles and miles of sea.'
Said one: 'Before the turn of tide
    We will achieve the eyrie-seat.'
Said one: 'Tomorrow shall be like
    Today, but much more sweet.'

'Tomorrow,' said they, strong with hope,
    And dwelt upon the pleasant way:
'Tomorrow,' cried they one and all,
    While no one spoke of yesterday.
Their life stood full at blessed noon;
    I, only I, had passed away:
'Tomorrow and today,' they cried;
    I was of yesterday.

I shivered comfortless, but cast
    No chill across the tablecloth;
I all-forgotten shivered, sad
    To stay and yet to part how loth:
I passed from the familiar room,
    I who from love had passed away,
Like the remembrance of a guest
    That tarrieth but a day.

THE SHORTEST AND SWEETEST
OF SONGS

Come
Home.

HAPPY FAMILIES

The stick-together families are happier by far . . .

EDGAR GUEST

Sometimes one of them leaves the house on a stretcher . . .

LISEL MUELLER

HAPPINESS

lying in bed ofa weekdaymorning
Autumn
and the trees
none the worse for it.
Youve just got up
to make tea toast and a bottle
leaving pastures warm
for me to stretch into

in his cot
the littlefella
outsings the birds

Plenty of honey in the cupboard.
Nice.

ROGER McGOUGH (1937−)

BREAKFAST

He put the coffee
In the cup
He put the milk
In the cup of coffee
He put the sugar
In the *café au lait*
With the coffee spoon

He stirred
He drank the *café au lait*
And he set down the cup
Without a word to me
He lit
A cigarette
He made smoke-rings
With the smoke
He put the ashes
In the ash-tray
Without a word to me
Without a look at me
He got up
He put
His hat upon his head
He put his raincoat on
Because it was raining
And he left
In the rain
Without a word
Without a look at me
And I   I took
My head in my hand
And I cried.

JACQUES PRÉVERT (1900–77)
TR. LAWRENCE FERLINGHETTI

FORTUNATI NIMIUM

Jacke and Jone they thinke no ill,
But loving live, and merry still;
Do their weeke-dayes' worke, and pray
Devotely on the holy day:
Skip and trip it on the greene,
And help to chuse the Summer Queene;
Lash out, at a Country Feast,
Their silver penny with the best.

Well can they judge of nappy Ale,
And tell at large a Winter tale;
Climbe up to the Apple loft,
And turne the crabs till they be soft.
Tib is all the father's joy,
And little Tom the mother's boy.
All their pleasure is Content;
And care, to pay their yearely rent.

Jone can call by name her Cowes,
And decke her windows with greene boughs;
Shee can wreathes and tuttyes make,
And trimme with plums a Bridall Cake.
Jacke knowes what brings gaine or losse;
And his long Flaile can stoutly tosse,
Make the hedge which others break,
And ever thinkes what he doth speake.

Now you Courtly Dames and Knights,
That study onely strange delights;

Though you scorn the homespun gray,
And revell in your rich array:
Though your tongues dissemble deepe,
And can your heads from danger keepe;
Yet for all your pomp and traine,
Securer lives the silly Swaine.

THOMAS CAMPION (1567–1620)

From MODERN LOVE

At dinner, she is hostess, I am host.
Went the feast ever cheerfuller? She keeps
The Topic over intellectual deeps
In buoyancy afloat. They see no ghost.
With sparkling surface-eyes we ply the ball:
It is in truth a most contagious game;
HIDING THE SKELETON shall be its name.
Such play as this the devils might appal!
But here's the greater wonder; in that we,
Enamour'd of our acting and our wits,
Admire each other like true hypocrites.
Warm-lighted looks, Love's Ephemerae,
Shoot gaily o'er the dishes and the wine.
We waken envy of our happy lot.
Fast, sweet, and golden, shows our marriage-knot.
Dear guests, you now have seen Love's corpse-light
        shine.

BEING BORING

'May you live in interesting times.' Chinese curse

If you ask me 'What's new?', I have nothing to say
Except that the garden is growing.
I had a slight cold but it's better today.
I'm content with the way things are going.
Yes, he is the same as he usually is,
Still eating and sleeping and snoring.
I get on with my work. He gets on with his.
I know this is all very boring.

There was drama enough in my turbulent past:
Tears and passion – I've used up a tankful.
No news is good news, and long may it last.
If nothing much happens, I'm thankful.
A happier cabbage you never did see,
My vegetable spirits are soaring.
If you're after excitement, steer well clear of me.
I want to go on being boring.

I don't go to parties. Well, what are they for,
If you don't need to find a new lover?
You drink and you listen and drink a bit more
And you take the next day to recover.
Someone to stay home with was all my desire
And, now that I've found a safe mooring,
I've just one ambition in life: I aspire
To go on and on being boring.

HAPPY AND UNHAPPY FAMILIES I

If all happy families are alike,
then so are the unhappy families,
who lives we celebrate
because they are motion and heat,
because they are what we think of as *life*.
Someone is lying and someone else
is being lied to. Someone is beaten
and someone else is doing the beating.
Someone is praying, or weeps
because she does not know how to pray.
Someone drinks all night;
someone cowers in corners;
someone threatens and someone pleads.
Bitter words at the table,
bitter sobs in the bedroom;
reprisal breathed on the bathroom mirror.
The house crackles with secrets;
everyone draws up a plan of escape.
Somebody shatters without a sound.
Sometimes one of them leaves the house
on a stretcher, in terrible silence.
How much energy suffering takes!
It is like a fire that burns and burns
but cannot burn down to extinction.
Unhappy families are never idle;
they are where the action is,
unlike the others, the happy ones,

who never raise their voices
and spit no blood, who do nothing
to deserve their happiness.

LISEL MUELLER (1924–2000)

ON AN UNSOCIABLE FAMILY

O what a strange parcel of creatures are we,
Scarce ever to quarrel, or ever agree;
We all are alone, though at home altogether,
Except to the fire constrain'd by the weather;
Then one says, 'tis cold, which we all of us know,
And with unanimity answer, 'tis so:
With shrugs and with shivers all look at the fire,
And shuffle ourselves and our chairs a bit nigher;
Then quickly, preceded by silence profound,
A yawn epidemical catches around:
Like social companions we never fall out,
Nor ever care what one another's about;
To comfort each other is never our plan,
For to please ourselves, truly, is more than we can.

ELIZABETH HANDS (1746–1815)   101

MY FAMILY'S FOND OF GADGETS

My family's fond of gadgets
and new technology.
My mother likes her radio.
My father likes TV.

My sister likes to dance around
the house with headphones on.
My brother plays on his PC
until the break of dawn.

The baby has a smartphone
and a touchscreen-tablet too.
If we had pets, I'm sure
that even they would have a few.

We chat with instant messaging.
We email and we text.
We're always looking forward
to the gadget we'll get next.

The power went out recently.
That day was like no other.
Our screens went blank and, strange but true,
we talked to one another.

WHERE CHILDREN LIVE

Homes where children live exude a pleasant
        rumpledness,
like a bed made by a child, or a yard littered with
        balloons.

To be a child again one would need to shed details
till the heart found itself dressed in the coat with
        a hood.
Now the heart has taken on gloves and mufflers,
the heart never goes outside to find something to do.
And the house takes on a new face, dignified.
No lost shoes blooming under bushes.
No chipped trucks in the drive.
Grown-ups like swings, leafy plants, slow-motion
        back and forth.
While the yard of a child is strewn with the corpses
of bottle-rockets and whistles,
anything whizzing and spectacular, brilliantly
        short-lived.

Trees in children's yards speak in clearer tongues.
Ants have more hope. Squirrels dance as well as hide.
The fence has a reason to be there, so children can go
        in and out.
Even when the children are at school, the yards glow
with the leftovers of their affection,
the roots of the tiniest grasses curl toward one another
like secret smiles.

FATHER IN FRONT OF A PICTURE

Vermeer's girl leans her sleeping head
on the neat curve of a wristbone, her
propped elbow taking the weight. Warm
fleshlight and lived-in familial shade
share the open doorway and watch over her
like a father, I imagine, while she snatches
brief sleep, and dreams he'll be
standing in her light when she wakes.

This agate-keen December day – a few
green streaks of grass breaking the bleak
amnesia of snow; nuthatches, finches,
chickadees quick as spring in the famished
branches – I must imagine how my own two children
will grow to know my absence
like a hint of pipe tobacco fading
as you enter a familiar room, like
a light on the landing gone out before you've
quite dropped into sleep and you lie
alone in the dark and know the dark
disputed borders of yourself, your self,
for the first time. How their sleep-warm

skin shivered when I came home
cold from my early-morning walks
this time of year, nuzzling them awake
with my rimey beard and the names of birds
I'd seen – a frost-edge glitter of wingtip

and tailfeather springing to sudden life in that
drowsy room. No knowing whether they'll
ever remember such mornings, now we're
separate, or know only my absence like
warm light bulging an open doorway while
they wish themselves to sleep, to dream
me there watching them all night until they wake
and with their own eyes find me, large as life.

EAMON GRENNAN (1941–)

SESTINA

September rain falls on the house.
In the failing light, the old grandmother
sits in the kitchen with the child
beside the Little Marvel Stove,
reading the jokes from the almanac,
laughing and talking to hide her tears.

She thinks that her equinoctial tears
and the rain that beats on the roof of the house
were both foretold by the almanac,
but only known to a grandmother.
The iron kettle sings on the stove.
She cuts some bread and says to the child,

It's time for tea now; but the child
is watching the teakettle's small hard tears
dance like mad on the hot black stove,
the way the rain must dance on the house.
Tidying up, the old grandmother
hangs up the clever almanac

on its string. Birdlike, the almanac
hovers half open above the child,
hovers above the old grandmother
and her teacup full of dark brown tears.
She shivers and says she thinks the house
feels chilly, and puts more wood in the stove.

It was to be, says the Marvel Stove.
I know what I know, says the almanac.
With crayons the child draws a rigid house
and a winding pathway. Then the child
puts in a man with buttons like tears
and shows it proudly to the grandmother.

But secretly, while the grandmother
busies herself about the stove,
the little moons fall down like tears
from between the pages of the almanac
into the flower bed the child
has carefully placed in the front of the house.

Time to plant tears, says the almanac.
The grandmother sings to the marvellous stove
and the child draws another inscrutable house.

A HOUSE OF MERCY

It was a house of female habitation,
Two ladies fair inhabited the house,
And they were brave. For although Fear
      knocked loud
Upon the door, and said he must come in,
They did not let him in.

There were also two feeble babes, two girls,
That Mrs S. had by her husband had,
He soon left them and went away to sea,
Nor sent them money, nor came home again
Except to borrow back
Her Naval Officer's Wife's Allowance from Mrs S.
Who gave it him at once, she thought she should.

There was also the ladies' aunt
And babes' great aunt, a Mrs Martha Hearn Clode,
And she was elderly.
These ladies put their money all together
And so we lived.

I was the younger of the feeble babes
And when I was a child my mother died
And later Great Aunt Martha Hearn Clode died
And later still my sister went away.

Now I am old I tend my mother's sister
The noble aunt who so long tended us,
Faithful and True her name is. Tranquil.
Also Sardonic. And I tend the house.

It is a house of female habitation
A house expecting strength as it is strong
A house of aristocratic mould that looks apart
When tears fall; counts despair
Derisory. Yet it has kept us well. For all its faults,
If they are faults, of sternness and reserve,
It is a Being of warmth I think; at heart
A house of mercy.

ABOUT THE HOUSE

There is nothing like staying at home for real comfort.

JANE AUSTEN

THE DOOR

Too little
has been said
of the door, its one
face turned to the night's
downpour and its other
to the shift and glisten of firelight.

Air, clasped
by this cover
into the room's book,
is filled by the turning
pages of dark and fire
as the wind shoulders the panels, or unsteadies
       that burning.

Not only
the storm's
breakwater, but the sudden
frontier to our concurrences, appearances,
and as full of the offer of space
as the view through a cromlech is.

For doors
are both frame and monument
to our spent time,
and too little
has been said
of our coming through and leaving by them.

CHARLES TOMLINSON (1927–2015)   111

LOVE IN A LIFE

Room after room,
I hunt the house through
We inhabit together.
Heart, fear nothing, for, heart, thou shalt find her –
Next time, herself! – not the trouble behind her
Left in the curtain, the couch's perfume!
As she brushed it, the cornice-wreath blossomed anew:
Yon looking-glass gleamed at the wave of her feather.

Yet the day wears,
And door succeeds door;
I try the fresh fortune –
Range the wide house from the wing to the centre.
Still the same chance! she goes out as I enter.
Spend my whole day in the quest, – who cares?
But 'tis twilight, you see, – with such suites to explore,
Such closets to search, such alcoves to importune!

ROBERT BROWNING (1812–89)

THE SUNNE RISING

Busie old foole, unruly Sunne,
Why dost thou thus,
Through windowes, and through curtaines call on us?
Must to thy motions lovers seasons run?

Sawcy pedantique wretch, goe chide
Late schoole boyes and sowre prentices,
Goe tell Court-huntsmen, that the King will ride,
Call countrey ants to harvest offices;
Love, all alike, no season knowes, nor clyme,
Nor houres, dayes, moneths, which are the rags of
time.

Thy beames, so reverend, and strong
Why shouldst thou thinke?
I could eclipse and cloud them with a winke,
But that I would not lose her sight so long:
If her eyes have not blinded thine,
Looke, and to morrow late, tell mee,
Whether both the'India's of spice and Myne
Be where thou leftst them, or lie here with mee.
Aske for those Kings whom thou saw'st yesterday,
And thou shalt heare, All here in one bed lay.

She'is all States, and all Princes, I,
Nothing else is.
Princes doe but play us, compar'd to this,
All honor's mimique; All wealth alchimie;
Thou sunne art halfe as happy'as wee,
In that the world's contracted thus.
Thine age askes ease, and since thy duties bee
To warme the world, that's done in warming us.
Shine here to us, and thou art every where;
This bed thy center is, these walls, thy spheare.

BATH

The day is fresh-washed and fair, and there is a smell of tulips and narcissus in the air.

The sunshine pours in at the bath-room window and bores through the water in the bath-tub in lathes and planes of greenish-white. It cleaves the water into flaws like a jewel, and cracks it to bright light.

Little spots of sunshine lie on the surface of the water and dance, dance, and their reflections wobble deliciously over the ceiling; a stir of my finger sets them whirring, reeling. I move a foot, and the planes of light in the water jar. I lie back and laugh, and let the green-white water, the sun-flawed beryl water, flow over me. The day is almost too bright to bear, the green water covers me from the too bright day. I will lie here awhile and play with the water and the sun spots.

The sky is blue and high. A crow flaps by the window, and there is a whiff of tulips and narcissus in the air.

LIVING ROOM

God sees me. I see you. You're just like me.
　　This is the cul-de-sac I've longed to live on.
Pure-white and dormered houses sit handsomely

along the slate-roofed, yew-lined neighborhood.
　　Past there is where my daughters walk to school,
across the common rounded by a wood.

And in my great room, a modest TV
　　informs me how the earth is grown so small,
ringed in spice routes of connectivity.

My father lived and died in his same chair
　　and kept it to one beer. There's good in that.
Who could look down upon, or even dare

to question, what he managed out of life?
　　Age makes us foolish. Still, he had a house,
a patch of grass and room to breathe, a wife.

It's my house now, and I do as I please.
　　I bless his name. I edge the yard, plant greens.
Our girls swing on the porch in a coming breeze.

WINTER'S SONG
From *Love's Labour's Lost*

When icicles hang by the wall,
    And Dick the shepherd blows his nail,
And Tom bears logs into the hall,
    And milk comes frozen home in pail,
When blood is nipped, and ways be foul,
Then nightly sings the staring owl,

                      'Tu-whit,
Tu-who!' a merry note,
While greasy Joan doth keel the pot.

When all aloud the wind doth blow,
    And coughing drowns the parson's saw,
And birds sit brooding in the snow,
    And Marian's nose looks red and raw,
When roasted crabs hiss in the bowl,
Then nightly sings the staring owl,

                      'Tu-whit,
Tu-who!' a merry note,
While greasy Joan doth keel the pot.

THIS IS JUST TO SAY

I have eaten
the plums
that were in
the icebox

and which
you were probably
saving
for breakfast

Forgive me
they were delicious
so sweet
and so cold

WILLIAM CARLOS WILLIAMS (1883–1963)

THE GEOGRAPHY OF THE HOUSE
(*for Christopher Isherwood*)

Seated after breakfast
In this white-tiled cabin
Arabs call *the House where
Everybody goes,*
Even melancholics

Raise a cheer to Mrs.
Nature for the primal
Pleasures she bestows.

Sex is but a dream to
Seventy-and-over,
But a joy proposed un-
     -til we start to shave:
Mouth-delight depends on
Virtue in the cook, but
This She guarantees from
Cradle unto grave.

Lifted off the potty,
Infants from their mothers
Hear their first impartial
Words of worldly praise:
Hence, to start the morning
With a satisfactory
Dump is a good omen
All our adult days.

Revelation came to
Luther in a privy
(Crosswords have been solved there):
Rodin was no fool
When he cast his Thinker,
Cogitating deeply,
Crouched in the position
Of a man at stool.

All the Arts derive from
This ur-act of making,
Private to the artist:
Makers' lives are spent
Striving in their chosen
Medium to produce a
De-narcissus-ized en-
   -during excrement.

Freud did not invent the
Constipated miser:
Banks have letter boxes
Built in their façade,
Marked *For Night Deposits*,
Stocks are firm or liquid,
Currencies of nations
Either soft or hard.

Global Mother, keep our
Bowels of compassion
Open through our lifetime,
Purge our minds as well:
Grant us a kind ending,
Not a second childhood,
Petulant, weak-sphinctered,
In a cheap hotel.

Keep us in our station:
When we get pound-noteish,
When we seem about to
Take up Higher Thought,
Send us some deflating
Image like the pained ex-
    -pression on a Major
Prophet taken short.

(Orthodoxy ought to
Bless our modern plumbing:
Swift and St Augustine
Lived in centuries,
When a stench of sewage
Ever in the nostrils
Made a strong debating
Point for Manichees.)

Mind and Body run on
Different timetables:
Not until our morning
Visit here can we
Leave the dead concerns of
Yesterday behind us,
Face with all our courage
What is now to be.

PERHAPS THE WORLD ENDS HERE

The world begins at a kitchen table. No matter what, we must eat to live.

The gifts of earth are brought and prepared, set on the table. So it has been since creation, and it will go on.

We chase chickens or dogs away from it. Babies teethe at the corners. They scrape their knees under it.

It is here that children are given instructions on what it means to be human. We make men at it, we make women.

At this table we gossip, recall enemies and the ghosts of lovers.

Our dreams drink coffee with us as they put their arms around our children. They laugh with us at our poor falling-down selves and as we put ourselves back together once again at the table.

This table has been a house in the rain, an umbrella in the sun.

Wars have begun and ended at this table. It is a place to hide in the shadow of terror. A place to celebrate the terrible victory.

We have given birth on this table, and have prepared our parents for burial here.

At this table we sing with joy, with sorrow. We pray of suffering and remorse. We give thanks.

Perhaps the world will end at the kitchen table, while we are laughing and crying, eating of the last sweet bite.

SPICK AND SPAN

All the ills of the world are only Untidiness, I decide.

GEORGE MacBETH

        Patching a tear
In the *kamiko*,
        With a few grains of cooked rice.

BUSON (1716–84)
TR. R. H. BLYTH

HOUSEHOLD HINTS

Old clothes have hearts, livers that last longer:
The veils, chemises, embroidered blouses
Brought back to life in suds and warm water,
Black lace revived by black tea, or crape
Passed to and fro through steam from a kettle.

So look on this as an antique nightdress
That has sleepwalked along hundreds of miles
Of rugs and carpets and linoleum,
Its clean hem lifted over the spilt milk
And ink, the occasional fall of soot.

This places you at a dressing-table,
Two sleeves that float into the looking-glass
Above combs and brushes, mother-of-pearl,
Tortoiseshell, silver, the discreet litter
Of your curling papers and crimping pins.

Though I picked it up for next to nothing
Wear this each night against your skin, accept

My advice about blood stains and mildew,
Cedar wood and camphor as protection
Against moths, alum-water against fire,

For I have been bruised like the furniture
And am more than a list of household hints,
The blackleader of stoves and bootscrapers,
Mender of sash cords, the mirror you slip
Between sheets to prove that the bed is damp.

MICHAEL LONGLEY (1939–)

WASHING-DAY

The Muses are turned gossips; they have lost
The buskined step, and clear high-sounding phrase,
Language of gods. Come then, domestic Muse,
In slipshod measure loosely prattling on
Of farm or orchard, pleasant curds and cream,
Or drowning flies, or shoe lost in the mire
By little whimpering boy, with rueful face;
Come, Muse, and sing the dreaded Washing-Day.
Ye who beneath the yoke of wedlock bend,
With bowed soul, full well ye ken the day
Which week, smooth sliding after week, brings on
Too soon; – for to that day nor peace belongs
Nor comfort; – ere the first grey streak of dawn,
The red-armed washers come and chase repose.

Nor pleasant smile, nor quaint device of mirth,
E'er visited that day; the very cat,
From the wet kitchen scared, and reeking hearth,
Visits the parlour, – an unwonted guest.
The silent breakfast-meal is soon despatched;
Uninterrupted, save by anxious looks
Cast at the lowering sky, if sky should lower.
From that last evil, O preserve us, heavens!
For should the skies pour down, adieu to all
Remains of quiet: then expect to hear
Of sad disasters, – dirt and gravel stains
Hard to efface, and loaded lines at once
Snapped short, – and linen-horse by dog
      thrown down,
And all the petty miseries of life.
Saints have been calm while stretched upon the rack,
And Guatimozin smiled on burning coals;
But never yet did housewife notable
Greet with a smile a rainy washing-day.
– But grant the welkin fair, require not thou
Who call'st thyself perchance the master there,
Or study swept, or nicely dusted coat,
Or usual 'tendance; – ask not, indiscreet,
Thy stockings mended, though the yawning rents
Gape wide as Erebus; nor hope to find
Some snug recess impervious: shouldst thou try
The 'customed garden walks, thine eye shall rue
The budding fragrance of thy tender shrubs,
Myrtle or rose, all crushed beneath the weight

Of coarse checked apron, – with impatient hand
Twitched off when showers impend: or crossing lines
Shall mar thy musings, as the wet cold sheet
Flaps in thy face abrupt. Woe to the friend
Whose evil stars have urged him forth to claim
On such a day the hospitable rites!
Looks, blank at best, and stinted courtesy,
Shall he receive. Vainly he feeds his hopes
With dinner of roast chickens, savoury pie,
Or tart or pudding: – pudding he nor tart
That day shall eat; nor, though the husband try,
Mending what can't be helped, to kindle mirth
From cheer deficient, shall his consort's brow
Clear up propitious: – the unlucky guest
In silence dines, and early slinks away.
I well remember, when a child, the awe
This day struck into me; for then the maids,
I scarce knew why, looked cross, and drove me
          from them:
Nor soft caress could I obtain, nor hope
Usual indulgencies; jelly or creams,
Relic of costly suppers, and set by
For me their petted one; or buttered toast,
When butter was forbid; or thrilling tale
Of ghost or witch, or murder – so I went
And sheltered me beside the parlour fire:
There my dear grandmother, eldest of forms,
Tended the little ones, and watched from harm,
Anxiously fond, though oft her spectacles

With elfin cunning hid, and oft the pins
Drawn from her ravelled stockings, might
        have soured
One less indulgent. –
At intervals my mother's voice was heard,
Urging despatch: briskly the work went on,
All hands employed to wash, to rinse, to wring,
To fold, and starch, and clap, and iron, and plait.
Then would I sit me down, and ponder much
Why washings were. Sometimes through
        hollow bowl
Of pipe amused we blew, and sent aloft
The floating bubbles; little dreaming then
To see, Montgolfier, thy silken ball
Ride buoyant through the clouds – so near approach
The sports of children and the toils of men.
Earth, air, and sky, and ocean, hath its bubbles,
And verse is one of them – this most of all.

ANNA LAETITIA BARBAULD (1743 – 1825)

IRONING

I used to iron everything:
my iron flying over sheets and towels
like a sledge chased by wolves over snow,

the flex twisting and crinking
until the sheath frayed, exposing
wires like nerves. I stood like a horse

with a smoking hoof
inviting anyone who dared
to lie on my silver-padded board,

to be pressed to the thinness
of dolls cut from paper.
I'd have commandeered a crane

if I could, got the welders at Jarrow
to heat me an iron the size of a tug
to flatten the house.

Then for years I ironed nothing.
I put the iron in a high cupboard.
I converted to crumpledness.

And now I iron again: shaking
dark spots of water onto wrinkled
silk, nosing into sleeves, round

buttons, breathing the sweet heated smell
hot metal draws from newly-washed
cloth, until my blouse dries

to a shining, creaseless blue,
an airy shape with room to push
my arms, breasts, lungs, heart into.

From TUPPERWARE SONNETS

I

I just love my Happy Chopper. It's just brilliant.
I don't know where I'd be now without it, without my
    Happy Chopper. I love it.
I have two. I have two Happy Choppers.
That way I always have a clean Happy Chopper. Even
    when I haven't done the dishes.
Can I demonstrate the Happy Chopper? It's so easy.
You just snap on the lid, and twist, and chop.
Look, you can even use your Happy Chopper while
    you're holding the baby.
One-handed. Just like this. I love my Happy Chopper.
I use it for mooshing up Billie's food. When it's not
    small enough.
You know how some of them have really big chunks?
I don't like to give her chunks.
I use my Happy Chopper on raw chicken. I just hate
    touching raw chicken.
It's great for guacamole too – you don't get slimies on
    your fingers.
I use mine to make nice little portions of chocolate.
    Happy chocolate. Guilt-free.
And it means you don't cry over onions.

. . .

IV

What about the Munchettes? Tell the ladies about
      those.

Oh, the Munchette containers are great.

They've got nice big tops, so kids can get their little
      hands in.

And a line here, so you know how far to fill them,
      how many sultanas they should eat.

And they're airtight, water-tight, you don't need
      plastic.

No plastic? But what about their sandwiches?

No, you don't need plastic on their sandwiches.

Don't they go yuck? I mean, I hate using plastic, but
      always worry,

won't their sandwiches go yuck? They won't eat their
      sandwiches if they go yuck.

They're in the bag all day, they must go yuck without
      the plastic.

The Munchette keeps everything crisp and fresh and
      clean. I don't use plastic any more.

Even tomato? Tomato sauce? My Kylie loves devon
      and tomato sauce.

Or cottage cheese and lettuce. They'd go yuck.
      Without the plastic.

That's the great thing about this range, you don't
      need any plastic.

You're saving the environment as well.

DUSTING

Thank you for these tiny
particles of ocean salt,
pearl-necklace viruses,
winged protozoans:
for the infinite,
intricate shapes
of submicroscopic
living things.

For algae spores
and fungus spores,
bonded by vital
mutual genetic cooperation,
spreading their
inseparable lives
from equator to pole.

My hand, my arm,
make sweeping circles.
Dust climbs the ladder of light.
For this infernal, endless chore,
for these eternal seeds of rain:
Thank you. For dust.

MARILYN NELSON (1946–)

Year's end,
all corners
of this floating world, swept.

BASHO (1644–94)
TR. LUCIEN STRYK AND TAKASHI IKEMOTO

A TIDY POEM ON UNTIDINESS

Untidiness is taking over.

For instance:
> Untidiness had marmalade for breakfast. It put
> its tongue in the jar and licked the undersides
> of my table.
> Untidiness came down the chimney and left its
> toys on the hearth.
> Untidiness has a bowel complaint. It did its
> business, more than once, in the drawing-room
> last night.

Untidiness is my friend. It puts its toe round the door
> and offers me toffee wrappers.

Untidiness, please go and play in another room.
> Another house. Out in the garden, maybe.

No! Not in the garden. (Untidiness, I remember, has
> already rolled its broken gutter pipes in the
> leaves below the beech-tree.)

Go home, Untidiness. Go round and have some fun at
the farm. You don't live here.

O, dear. Untidiness, I believe you. I saw the room
with the Gothic fire just now and the state of
its bed linen.

So when did I beget you? Surely it wasn't me. I must
have been out of my mind.

Unshapely Untidiness, I readily don't adore your
games. Will you take a break? Have a vacation.
Go to Waxham for the day.

Yes. Who is it? O, really, is that so? I dream
Untidiness went down to the beach and
dropped my property file in the sea. (It also left
its pebbles in the boot of my car.)

Untidiness, I'm sorry. I see that you're really mine.
I have to accept your presence, and your
presents.

I lie back. I sniff the air. I try to enjoy the stale odour
of spilled milk from the sofa. I make a virtue
out of the broken plastic flower pots in the
rockery. I drink in the unwashed laundry on
the first floor landing. I become a connoisseur
of dust on window-sills.

All the ills of the world are only Untidiness, I decide.

I become a martyr to Untidiness.

I wear an unironed shirt. I put on odd socks. I steam
    in wet underpants.

Goodnight, Untidiness. I'm tired. I'm going to bed.
    Sleep well, old monster.

I climb the stairs to my bedroom. Alas, Untidiness
    has got there first. The tins of paint and their
    dripping brushes already create an elaborate
    smear by my slippers.

Enough. Untidiness must stop! I fill my drawers with
    a jumble of papers and clothes. I sink back,
    exhausted, on my unmade bed.

As I fall asleep, I hear Untidiness as it drips from the
    kitchen tap.

It lulls me, Untidiness. It lulls me. It lulls me to sleep.

WHAT, IN OUR HOUSE?

'The play (*Macbeth*) is remarkably short, and it may be there has been some cutting.' J. G. Collingwood

MACDUFF   O Banquo, Banquo,
  Our royal master's murdered.
LADY MACBETH   Woe, alas!
  What, in our house?
BANQUO   Too cruel anywhere.
LADY MACBETH That's not the point. Who cares
    for anywhere?
  Mere woolly-minded liberals. But *here*
  Is where I am, my house, my place, my world,
  My fortress against time and dirt and things.
  Here I deploy my garrison of soap,
  And, like all housewives, just about contrive
  To outmanoeuvre chaos. Not a job
  For men. What man alive will grovel
  Scrubbing at floorboards to mop up the blood?
  (No doubt there's blood? Or if not, sick or shit
  Or other filth that women have to handle?)
BANQUO O gentle lady . . .
LADY MACBETH   Only women know
  The quantity of blood there is that waits
  To flood from bodies; how it soaks and seeps
  In wood and wool and walls, and stains for ever.
  No disinfectant, I can tell you, Banquo,
  So strong as blood. Then, the implicit slur

Upon my hospitality. Was Duncan
Suffocated? Something wrong with the pillows!
Was his throat cut? Check the carving knives!
Poison? Blame the cuisine. I wish to heaven,
Banquo, he'd died in *your* house. Your wife
Would tell you how I feel.

Enter Malcolm and Donalbain

DONALBAIN   What is amiss?
MACDUFF Your royal father's murdered.
MALCOLM   O, by whom?

LADY MACBETH Such donnish syntax at so grave
    a moment!
  How hard to frame the first and random thought
  Detection snuffs at, to seem innocent
  And psycholinguistically correct at once.
  And my *best* bedroom, too.

A WOMAN'S PLACE

Are we not homes? And is not all therein?
Wring the world dry to meet our wide desires!
We crown all life! We are the aim of God!

CHARLOTTE PERKINS GILMAN

You'd be so nice to come home to . . .

COLE PORTER

HOUSEWIFE

Some women marry houses.
It's another kind of skin; it has a heart,
a mouth, a liver and bowel movements.
The walls are permanent and pink.
See how she sits on her knees all day,
faithfully washing herself down.
Men enter by force, drawn back like Jonah
into their fleshy mothers.
A woman *is* her mother.
That's the main thing.

From SHAKESPEARIAN READINGS

Oh, but to fade, and live we know not where,
To be a cold obstruction and to groan!
This sensible, warm woman, to become
A prudish clod; and the delighted spirit
To live and die alone, or to reside
With married sisters, and to have the care
Of half a dozen children, not your own;
And driven, for no one wants you,
Round about the pendant world; or worse than worst
Of those that disappointment and pure spite
Have driven to madness: 'T is too horrible!
The weariest and most troubled married life
That age, ache, penury, or jealousy
Can lay on nature, is a paradise
To being an old maid.

*

My father had a daughter got a man,
As it might be, perhaps, were I good-looking,
I should, your lordship.
And what's her residence?
A hut, my lord, she never owned a house,
But let her husband, like a graceless scamp,
Spend all her little means, – she thought she ought, –
And in a wretched chamber, on an alley,
She worked like masons on a monument,
Earning their bread. Was not this love indeed?

From BALLAD OF A TYRANNICAL HUSBAND

A medieval housewife 'ffayre and bold' confronts her angry husband, returned from a morning's ploughing to find no dinner on the table.

Then sware the goodwyff, and thus gane she say,
'I have mor to doo than doo I may;
And ye shuld folowe me ffoly on day,
Ye wold be wery off your part, my hede dar I lay.'

'Wery! yn the devylles nam!' seyd the goodman,
'What hast thou to doo, but syttes her at hame?
Thou goyst to thi neybores howse, be on and be one,
And syttes ther janglynge with Jake an with John.'

Than sayd the goodwyffe, 'feyr mot yow ffaylle!
I have mor to do, who so wyst alle;
Whyn I lye in my bede, my slepe is butt smalle,
Yett eyrly in the morneng ye wylle me up calle.

'Whan I lye al nyght wakyng with our cheylde,
I ryse up at morow and fynde owr howse wylde;
Then I melk owre kene and torne them on the felde,
Whylle yow slepe ffulle stylle, also Cryst me schelde!

'Than make I buter ferther on the day;
After make I chese, – thes holde yow a play;
Then wylle owre cheldren wepe and upemost they,
Yett wylle yow blame me for owr goods, and any
        be awey.

'Whan I have so done, yet ther comys more eene,
I geve our chekyns met, or elles they wylb[e] leyne:
Our hennes, our capons, and owr dokkes be-dene,
Yet tend I to owr goslyngs that gothe on the grene.

'I bake, I brew, yt wylle not elles be welle;
I bete and swyngylle flex, as ever have I heylle,
I hekylle the towe, I kave and I keylle,
I toose owlle and card het and spyn het on the wheylle.'

'Dame,' sed the goodman, 'the develle have thy bones!
Thou nedyst not bake nor brew in fortynght past onys;
I sey no good that thou dost within thes wyd wonys,
But ever thow excusyst the with grontes and gronys.'

. . . 'Whan I have so donne, I loke on the sonne,
I ordene met for owr bestes agen that yow come home,
And met ffor owr selfe agen het be none,
Yet I have not a ffeyr word whan I have done.

'Soo I loke to owr good withowt and withyn,
That ther be none awey noder mor nor myn,
Glade to ples yow to pay, lest any bate begyn,
And fort to chid thus with me, i-feyght yow be in synne.'

Then sed the goodman in a sory tyme,
'Alle thys wold a good howsewyf do long ar het wer
          prime;
And sene the good that we have is halfe dele thyn,
Thow shalt laber for thy part as I doo for myne.

'Therffor, dame, make the redy, I warne the, anone,
To morow with my lade to the plowe thou shalt gone;
And I wylbe howsewyfe and kype owr howse at home,
And take myn ese as thou hast done, by God and
    Seint John!'

The MSS breaks off as the wife sets off the next morning,
'courteous and capable'; it is clear that she will have no problem
with handling a plough. The tyrannical husband, on the other
hand, will be a domestic disaster (she has secretly taken a few
advance measures to make doubly sure of it!).

ANON. (late 15th century)

'HOW MANY TIMES THESE LOW FEET STAGGERED –'

How many times these low feet staggered –
Only the soldered mouth can tell –
Try – can you stir the awful rivet –
Try – can you lift the hasps of steel!

Stroke the cool forehead – hot so often –
Lift – if you care – the listless hair –
Handle the adamantine fingers
Never a thimble – more – shall wear –

Buzz the dull flies – on the chamber window –
Brave – shines the sun through the freckled pane –
Fearless – the cobweb swings from the ceiling –
Indolent Housewife – in Daisies – lain!

EMILY DICKINSON (1830–86)

WOMAN IN KITCHEN

Breakfast over, islanded by noise,
She watches the machines go fast and slow.
She stands among them as they shake the house.
They move; their destination is specific.
She has nowhere definite to go.
She might be a pedestrian in traffic.

White surfaces retract; white
Sideboards light the white of walls.
Cups wink white in their saucers.
The light of day bleaches as it falls
On cups and sideboards. She could use
The room to tap with if she lost her sight.

Machines jigsaw everything she knows
And she is everywhere among their furor:
The tropic of the dryer tumbling clothes,
The round lunar window of the washer.
The kettle in the toaster is a kingfisher
Roving for trout above the river's mirror.

The wash done, the kettle boiled, the sheets
Spun and clean, the dryer stops dead.
The silence is a death: it starts to bury
The room in white spaces. She turns to spread
A cloth on the board and irons sheets
In a room white and quiet as a mortuary.

From AURORA LEIGH

I had a little chamber in the house,
As green as any privet-hedge a bird
Might choose to build in, though the nest itself
Could show but dead-brown sticks and straws;
     the walls
Were green, the carpet was pure green, the straight
Small bed was curtained greenly, and the folds
Hung green about the window which let in
The outdoor world with all its greenery.
You could not push your head out and escape
A dash of dawn-dew from the honeysuckle,
But so you were baptised into the grace
And privilege of seeing . . .

I read books bad and good – some bad and good
At once (good aims not always make good books:
Well-tempered spades turn up ill-smelling soils
In digging vineyards even); books that prove
God's being so definitely, that man's doubt
Grows self-defined the other side the line,
Made atheist by suggestion; moral books,
Exasperating to license; genial books,
Discounting from the human dignity;
And merry books, which set you weeping when
The sun shines – ay, and melancholy books,
Which make you laugh that any one should weep
In this disjointed life for one wrong more.

The world of books is still the world, I write,
And both worlds have God's providence, thank God,
To keep and hearten . . .
                              But I could not hide
My quickening inner life from those at watch.
They saw a light at a window now and then,
They had not set there: who had set it there?
My father's sister started when she caught
My soul agaze in my eyes. She could not say
I had no business with a sort of soul,
But plainly she objected – and demurred,
That souls were dangerous things to carry straight
Through all the spilt saltpetre of the world.

She said sometimes, 'Aurora, have you done
Your task this morning? have you read that book?
And are you ready for the crochet here?' –
As if she said, 'I know there's something wrong;
I know I have not ground you down enough
To flatten and bake you to a wholesome crust
For household uses and proprieties,
Before the rain has got into my barn
And set the grains a-sprouting. What, you're green
With outdoor impudence? you almost grow?'

SAPPHO BURNS HER BOOKS AND CULTIVATES THE CULINARY ARTS

[On Miss R. P.'s Saying she would find Love only if she did so]

Companions of my favourite hours,
By Winter's fire, in Summer's bowers;
That wont to chase my bosom's care,
And plant your pleasing visions there!
Guarini, Dante, honour'd names!
Ah, doom'd to feed devouring flames!
Alas! my Petrarch's gentle loves!
My Tasso's rich enchanted groves!
My Ariosto's fairy dreams,
And all my lov'd Italian themes!
I saw you on the pile expire,
Weeping I saw the invading fire;
There fix'd remain'd my aching sight,
Till the last ray of parting light,
The last pale flame consum'd away,
And all dissolv'd – your relicks lay.

    Goddess of Culinary Art,
Now take possession of my heart!
Teach me more winning arts to try,
To salt the ham, to mix the pie;
To make the paste both light and thin,
To smooth it with the rolling-pin;
With taper skewer to print it round,
Lest ruder touch the surface wound.

Then teach thy votary how to make
That fair rotundo – a plumb cake;
To shake the compound sweets together,
To bake it light as any feather,
That when complete its form may show,
A rising hillock topped with snow;
And how to make the cheese-cake say,
To beat the eggs, and turn the whey;
To strain my jelly fair and clear,
That there no *misty fog* appear;
But plain to view each form may rise,
That in its glassy bosom lies.

Now fancy soars to future times,
When all extinct are Sappho's rhimes;
When none but Cooks applaud her name,
And nought but recipes' her fame.
When sweetest numbers she'll despise,
And Pope shall sing beneath *minced-pies*,
And Eloise in her *tin* shall mourn,
Disastrous fate and love forlorn;
Achilles too, that godlike man,
Shall bluster in the *patty-pan*;
And many a once-lov'd Grecian chief,
Shall guard from flames the roasting beef.

Then when this transformation's made,
And Sappho's vestments speak her *trade*;
When girt in towels she is seen,
With cuffs to keep her elbows clean:

Then Sorceress she'll call on thee!
Accomplish thou thy fair decree!
If like your sisters of the heath,
Whose mystic sound betray'd Macbeth;
Fallacious charms your arts dispense,
To cheat her with ambiguous sense;
Severest torments may you prove!
Severest – disappointed love.

From A SINGLE WOMAN'S BEDROOM

Turkish Bath

The room is choked with nudes.
Once, a man muscled in by mistake
Crying, 'Turkish bath!' He had no idea
My door is always locked in this heat,
No idea that I am the sole guest and client,
The chief consort, that I cast my gaze
Of pity and absolute pride across
The length of my limbs – pristine, lithe –
The bells of my breasts singing,
The high bright note of my ass,
My shoulders a warm chord,
The chorus of muscle that rings
Ecstatic. I am my own model.
I create, am created, my bed
Is heaped with photo albums,
Socks and slips scattered on a table.
A spray of winter jasmine wilts
In its glass vase, dim yellow, like
Despondent gold. Blossoms carpet
The floor, which is a patchwork
Of pillows. Pick a corner, sleep in peace.
　　You didn't come to live with me.

The curtain seals in my joy

The curtain seals out the day.
Better that way to let my mind
See what it sees (every evil under the sun),
Or to kneel before the heart, quiet king,
Feeling brave and consummately free.
Better that way to let all that I want
And all I believe swarm me like bees,
Or ghosts, or a cloud of smoke someone
Blows, beckoning. I come. I cry out
In release. I give birth
To a battery of clever babies – triplets,
Quintuplets, so many all at once.
The curtain seals in my joy.
The curtain holds the razor out of reach,
Puts the pills on a shelf out of sight.
The curtain snuffs shut and I bask in the bounty
Of being alive. The music begins.
Love pools in every corner.
     You didn't come to live with me.

Hope Beyond Hope

This city of riches has fallen empty.
Small rooms like mine are easy to breach.
Watchmen pace, peer in, gazes hungry.
I come and go, always alone, heavy with worry.
My flesh forsakes itself. Strangers' eyes
Drill into me till I bleed. I beg God:
Make me a ghost.
                        Fellow citizens:
Something invisible blocks every road.
I wait night after night with a hope beyond hope.
If you come, will nation rise against nation?
If you come, will the Yellow River drown its banks?
If you come, will the sky blacken and rage?
Will your coming decimate the harvest?
There is nothing I can do in the face of all I hate.
What I hate most is the person I've become.

    You didn't come to live with me.

YI LEI (1951–2018)
154   TR. TRACY K. SMITH AND CHANGTAI BI

VACANT POSSESSION

Homes of the loved ones, which are not homes
I see you as homes of the present absent.

AL–SANAWBARI

THE HOUSE ON THE HILL

They are all gone away,
   The House is shut and still,
There is nothing more to say.

Through broken walls and gray
   The winds blow bleak and shrill:
They are all gone away.

Nor is there one today
   To speak them good or ill:
There is nothing more to say.

Why is it then we stray
   Around the sunken sill?
They are all gone away.

And our poor fancy-play
   For them is wasted skill:
There is nothing more to say.

There is ruin and decay
   In the House on the Hill:
They are all gone away,
There is nothing more to say.

AN ABANDONED HUT

Those plum blossoms
We once floated in our wine.
Now the flowers are
Scattered, unnoticed,
All over the ground.

RYOKAN (1758–1831)
TR. JOHN STEVENS

LITTLE HOUSE, BIG HOUSE

In a day or two the chairs will fall to pieces:
Those who were once lovers need the minimum
Of furniture, half-people, each with his separate sky.

Christmas peered through the escallonia hedge,
And passed almost unnoticed, except the stamps
Had squirrels on them. Why should I take
My apron off for a wineless dinner? My things
Are too grey, like a tree I deepen shadows
With my brown autumn raincoat.

On the ground floor, one room opens into another,
And a small Matisse in the inglenook
Without its wood fire is stroked by light
From north and south. That started all the feelings
That had slept till then, I came out

From behind the tea-pot to find myself
Cooled by a new arrangement of doorways
And choosing a spiced bun from a china shell.

A shawl no whiter than my white skin
Made me a dust-jacket, I overwatered
The Michaelmas daisies thinking about
The claw-like bedroom door-handles along
The minstrel's gallery. And the house like me
Was tangled with the emotion of cut flowers –

So different from an ordinary going-away –
That I could hardly keep my hand
From phoning you, impromptu. Since our blood
Is always older than we will ever be,
I should like to lie in Tarusa under matted
        winter grass,
Where the strawberries are redder than
        anywhere else.

OLD WOMAN

So much she caused she cannot now account for
As she stands watching day return, the cool
Walls of the house moving towards the sun.
She puts some flowers in a vase and thinks
    'There is not much I can arrange
In here and now, but flowers are suppliant

As children never were. And love is now
A flicker of memory, my body is
My own entirely. When I lie at night
I gather nothing now into my arms,
    No child or man, and where I live
Is what remains when men and children go.'

Yet she owns more than residue of lives
That she has marked and altered. See how she
Warns time from too much touching her possessions
By keeping flowers fed, by polishing
    Her fine old silver. Gratefully
She sees her own glance printed on grandchildren.

Drawing the curtains back and opening windows
Every morning now, she feels her years
Grow less and less. Time puts no burden on
Her now she does not need to measure it.
    It is acceptance she arranges
And her own life she places in the vase.

AFTERMATH OF A DEPARTURE

When you left, you took with you
my wardrobe

That, and the kitchen, and the vegetable garden
and the gods in the room

Yesterday, I tripped on my saree
and ripped the edges of it. The 6 folds of cloth
tucked on my abdomen beneath the underskirt
came off and I stuffed it back in a hurry,
making it bulge out the rest of the day
Tie the skirt tight, tighter, I heard you say

I tried frying okras the way you did
It left a burning taste in my mouth, the taste
that reminded me of the year we went to Ooty
and had corn cob roasted on hot coal
You squeezed lemon on it to remove the bitterness
        of cinders,
a trick that might or might not work on my okras

I still take a bath first thing in the morning,
but the gods are always awake before me
I light the match stick
and extend my hands to the wick soaked in
        sesame oil,
The fan is turned off, the windows closed,
and I take care not to breathe
yet, somewhere on the way, the flame dies

And then there are the dents, two of them
on our plush sofa. One where you sat, peeling
        potatoes,
watching mega-serials of bad women scheming
        against good ones,
and the other where I did, fiddling with my laptop
Now I sit on the hump between the two dents
hoping that eventually the gaps would fill

These days, after I cook my lunch, burned or not
I leave a handful of rice on the backyard verandah
for the crows that are waiting to pounce on it;
all but one, who watches me astutely from the
        lowest branch
of the mango tree that you planted the year
        I was born.

And I know that is you,
watching out for me, telling me you are near.

From LETTER TO FERRANTE FRANCESCO D'AVALOS
(*Colonna's husband, after the Battle of Ravenna*)

My highest Lord, I am writing this letter
to tell you in what sadness I exist,
torn among doubt and loneliness and pain. . . .

When others asked for war, I called for peace,
sufficing me that my belovèd Marquis
should dwell with me content and satisfied.

Risky endeavors of war do not harm men;
but we women – afflicted and forsaken –
are hurt by fear and anxious care alike.

Compelled by your belligerence, you think
only of honor, and with loud war cries
you rush straight into the perils of battle.

But left behind, we, fearful and sad,
worry for you: the sister wants the brother,
the bride the bridegroom, and the mother her son.

Wretchedly lonely, I long for my husband,
for my father and son: I am at once
spouse, daughter, sister and aging mother. . . .

Independent you live, devoid of cares
and thinking only to gain fame and acclaim –
you do not care if I yearn for your love.

My face darkened by sadness and disdain,
I lie alone in a forsaken bed,
feeling hope intertwined with bitter pain,

    and tempering my sorrows with your joy.

VITTORIA COLONNA (1492–1547)
TR. LAURA ANNA STORTONI AND
MARY PRENTICE LILLIE   163

FORTY-ONE, ALONE, NO GERBIL

In the strange quiet, I realise
there's no one else in the house. No bucktooth
mouth pulls at a stainless-steel teat, no
hairy mammal runs on a treadmill –
Charlie is dead, the last of our children's half-
      children.
When our daughter found him lying in the shavings,
      trans-
mogrified backwards from a living body
into a bolt of rodent bread
she turned her back on early motherhood
and went on single, with nothing. Crackers,
Fluffy, Pretzel, Biscuit, Charlie,
buried on the old farm we bought
where she could know nature. Well, now she knows it
and it sucks. Creatures she loved, mobile and
needy, have gone down stiff and indifferent,
she will not adopt again though she cannot
have children yet, her body like a blueprint
of the understructure for a woman's body,
so now everything stops for a while,
now I must wait many years
to hear in this house again the faint
powerful call of a young animal.

CURTAINS

Putting up new curtains,
other windows intrude.
As though it is that first winter in Cambridge
when you and I had just moved in.
Now cold borscht alone in a bare kitchen.

What does it mean if I say this years later?

Listen, last night
I am on a crying jag
with my landlord, Mr. Tempesta.
I sneaked in two cats.
He screams, 'No pets! No pets!'
I become my Aunt Virginia,
proud but weak in the head.
I remember Anna Magnani.
I throw a few books. I shout.
He wipes his eyes and opens his hands.
OK OK keep the dirty animals
but no nails in the walls.
We cry together.
I am so nervous, he says.

I want to dig you up and say, look,
it's like the time, remember,
when I ran into our living room naked
to get rid of that fire inspector.

See what you miss by being dead?

WIND AND MIST

They met inside the gateway that gives the view,
A hollow land as vast as heaven. 'It is
A pleasant day, sir.' 'A very pleasant day.'
'And what a view here. If you like angled fields
Of grass and grain bounded by oak and thorn,
Here is a league. Had we with Germany
To play upon this board it could not be
More dear than April has made it with a smile.
The fields beyond that league close in together
And merge, even as our days into the past,
Into one wood that has a shining pane
Of water. Then the hills of the horizon –
That is how I should make hills had I to show
One who would never see them what hills were like.'
'Yes. Sixty miles of South Downs at one glance.
Sometimes a man feels proud at them, as if
He had just created them with one mighty thought.'
'That house, though modern, could not be better
         planned
For its position. I never liked a new
House better. Could you tell me who lives in it?'
'No one.' 'Ah – and I was peopling all
Those windows on the south with happy eyes,
The terrace under them with happy feet;
Girls –' 'Sir, I know. I know. I have seen that house
Through mist look lovely as a castle in Spain,
And airier. I have thought: " 'Twere happy there

To live." And I have laughed at that
Because I lived there then.' 'Extraordinary.'
'Yes, with my furniture and family
Still in it, I, knowing every nook of it
And loving none, and in fact hating it.'
'Dear me! How could that be? But pardon me.'
'No offence. Doubtless the house was not to blame,
But the eye watching from those windows saw,
Many a day, day after day, mist – mist
Like chaos surging back – and felt itself
Alone in all the world, marooned alone.
We lived in clouds, on a cliff's edge almost
(You see), and if clouds went, the visible earth
Lay too far off beneath and like a cloud.
I did not know it was the earth I loved
Until I tried to live there in the clouds
And the earth turned to cloud.' 'You had a garden
Of flint and clay, too.' 'True; that was real enough.
The flint was the one crop that never failed.
The clay first broke my heart, and then my back;
And the back heals not. There were other things
Real, too. In that room at the gable a child
Was born while the wind chilled a summer dawn:
Never looked grey mind on a greyer one
Than when the child's cry broke above the groans.'
'I hope they were both spared.' 'They were. Oh yes.
But flint and clay and childbirth were too real
For this cloud-castle. I had forgot the wind.
Pray do not let me get on to the wind.

You would not understand about the wind.
It is my subject, and compared with me
Those who have always lived on the firm ground
Are quite unreal in this matter of the wind.
There were whole days and nights when the wind
and I
Between us shared the world, and the wind ruled
And I obeyed it and forgot the mist.
My past and the past of the world were in the wind.
Now you will say that though you understand
And feel for me, and so on, you yourself
Would find it different. You are all like that
If once you stand here free from wind and mist:
I might as well be talking to wind and mist.
You would believe the house-agent's young man
Who gives no heed to anything I say.
Good morning. But one word. I want to admit
That I would try the house once more, if I could;
As I should like to try being young again.'

'I REMEMBER,
I REMEMBER . . .'

Dear home, thou scene of earliest hopes and joys
The least of which wronged Memory ever makes
Bitterer than all thine unremembered tears.

PERCY BYSSHE SHELLEY

Take your heart wherever it desires,
Your true love will, after all, always be your first love.
How numerous are the houses in which you will reside,
Yet, never will you cease to yearn for your first house.

ABU TAMMAM

THE SELF-UNSEEING

Here is the ancient floor,
Footworn and hollowed and thin,
Here was the former door
Where the dead feet walked in.

She sat here in her chair,
Smiling into the fire;
He who played stood there,
Bowing it higher and higher.

Childlike, I danced in a dream;
Blessings emblazoned that day;
Everything glowed with a gleam;
Yet we were looking away!

MY EARLY HOME

Here sparrows build upon the trees,
    And stockdove hides her nest;
The leaves are winnowed by the breeze
    Into a calmer rest;
The black-cap's song was very sweet,
    That used the rose to kiss;
It made the Paradise complete:
    My early home was this.

The red-breast from the sweetbriar bush
    Dropt down to pick the worm;
On the horse-chestnut sang the thrush,
    O'er the house where I was born;
The moonlight, like a shower of pearls,
    Fell o'er this 'bower of bliss',
And on the bench sat boys and girls:
    My early home was this.

The old house stooped just like a cave,
    Thatched o'er with mosses green;
Winter around the walls would rave,
    But all was calm within;
The trees are here all green agen,
    Here bees the flowers still kiss,
But flowers and trees seemed sweeter then:
    My early home was this.

WHEN I AM IN THE KITCHEN

I think about the past. I empty the ice-cube trays
crack crack cracking like bones, and I think
of decades of ice cubes and of John Cheever,
of Anne Sexton making cocktails, of decades
of cocktail parties, and it feels suddenly far
too lonely at my counter. Although I have on hooks
nearby the embroidered apron of my friend's
grandmother and one my mother made for me
for Christmas 30 years ago with gingham I had
coveted through my childhood. In my kitchen
I wield my great aunt's sturdy black-handled
soup ladle and spatula, and when I pull out
the drawer, like one in a morgue, I visit
the silverware of my husband's grandparents.
We never met, but I place this in my mouth
every day and keep it polished out of duty.
In the cabinets I find my godmother's
teapot, my mother's Cambridge glass goblets,
my mother-in-law's Franciscan plates, and here
is the cutting board my first husband parqueted
and two potholders I wove in grade school.
Oh the past is too much with me in the kitchen,
where I open the vintage metal recipe box,
robin's egg blue in its interior, to uncover
the card for Waffles, writ in my father's hand
reaching out from the grave to guide me
from the beginning, 'sift and mix dry ingredients'

with his note that this makes '3 waffles in our
large pan' and around that *our* an unbearable
round stain – of egg yolk or melted butter? –
that once defined a world.

JEANNE MARIE BEAUMONT (1954–)

REMEMBER GRANNY TROT'S
MULBERRY JAM?

That was in the days of the old strip road,
before the merger, before the quarry
started looking like my Dad; long before
the fighting. I am thinking of a time,
a time of syringa-berry battles
and the stink of crushed marigolds as we, Fred,
Tazwill, my sister Pat – maybe Bob
if it was school holidays – untangled
our childhood. Round and round the yard we rushed
until the landlocked sky shook starlings
out of its blue. Before the puff-adder
killed Joe; before Mom stopped making konfyt
from watermelon skins; before Joji
Sibanda (who taught me Sindebele
swear words) was put in jail. It was a time
of bulldogs, and chickens, and vegetables
from the garden: capsicums, horse-radish,
pumpkin . . . and fruit. Our paw-paws were sweeter

than sugar. Even our lemons were sweet.
Remember Granny Trot's mulberry jam?
That was before she started fading down
the distance of her colonial eyes;
before we moved on full tar to the house
in the village; before my Dad's profile
was blasted away; just before the land-mines
started to appear. Then Joe. Then the way
our St Joseph's lilies stopped making flowers.
It could have been the granite sand. It could
have been a hot October wind. It could
have been the rattle of choppers. It could
have been a time for lilies to sicken
in the gathering shriek of cicadas.

From IN MEMORIAM

Unwatch'd, the garden bough shall sway,
    The tender blossom flutter down,
    Unloved, that beech will gather brown,
This maple burn itself away;

Unloved, the sun-flower, shining fair,
    Ray round with flames her disk of seed,
    And many a rose-carnation feed
With summer spice the humming air;

Unloved, by many a sandy bar,
    The brook shall babble down the plain,
    At noon or when the lesser wain
Is twisting round the polar star;

Uncared for, gird the windy grove,
    And flood the haunts of hern and crake;
    Or into silver arrows break
The sailing moon in creek and cove;

Till from the garden and the wild
    A fresh association blow,
    And year by year the landscape grow
Familiar to the stranger's child;

As year by year the labourer tills
    His wonted glebe, or lops the glades;
    And year by year our memory fades
From all the circle of the hills.

*

We leave the well-beloved place
    Where first we gazed upon the sky;
    The roofs, that heard our earliest cry,
Will shelter one of stranger race.

We go, but ere we go from home,
    As down the garden-walks I move,
    Two spirits of a diverse love
Contend for loving masterdom.

One whispers, 'Here thy boyhood sung
    Long since its matin song, and heard
    The low love-language of the bird
In native hazels tassel-hung.'

The other answers, 'Yea, but here
    Thy feet have stray'd in after hours
    With thy lost friend among the bowers,
And this hath made them trebly dear.'

These two have striven half the day,
    And each prefers his separate claim,
    Poor rivals in a losing game,
That will not yield each other way.

I turn to go; my feet are set
    To leave the pleasant fields and farms;
    The mix in one another's arms
To one pure image of regret.

SHILLINGTON

The vacant lots are occupied, the woods
Diminish, Slate Hill sinks, beneath its crown
Of solvent homes, and marketable goods
On all sides crowd the good remembered town.

Returning, we find our snapshots inexact.
Perhaps a condition of being alive
Is that the clothes which, setting out, we packed
With love no longer fit when we arrive.

Yet sights that limited our truth were strange
To older eyes; the town that we have lost
Is being found by hands that still arrange
Horse-chestnut heaps and fingerpaint on frost.

Time shades these alleys; every pavement crack
Is mapped somewhere. A solemn concrete ball,
On the gatepost of a sold house, brings back
A waist leaning against a buckling wall.

The gutter-fires smoke, their burning done
Except for, fanned within, an orange feather;
We have one home, the first, and leave that one.
The having and leaving go on together.

I REMEMBER, I REMEMBER

Coming up England by a different line
For once, early in the cold new year,
We stopped, and, watching men with number-plates
Sprint down the platform to familiar gates,
'Why, Coventry!' I exclaimed. 'I was born here.'

I leant far out, and squinnied for a sign
That this was still the town that had been 'mine'
So long, but found I wasn't even clear
Which side was which. From where those
　　　　cycle-crates
Were standing, had we annually departed

For all those family hols? . . . A whistle went:
Things moved. I sat back, staring at my boots.
'Was that,' my friend smiled, 'where you "have
　　　　your roots"?'
No, only where my childhood was unspent,
I wanted to retort, just where I started:

By now I've got the whole place clearly charted.
Our garden, first: where I did not invent
Blinding theologies of flowers and fruits,
And wasn't spoken to by an old hat.
And here we have that splendid family

I never ran to when I got depressed,
The boys all biceps and the girls all chest,
Their comic Ford, their farm where I could be
'Really myself'. I'll show you, come to that,
The bracken where I never trembling sat,

Determined to go through with it; where she
Lay back, and 'all became a burning mist'.
And, in those offices, my doggerel
Was not set up in blunt ten-point, nor read
By a distinguished cousin of the mayor,

Who didn't call and tell my father *There*
Before us, had we the gift to see ahead –
'You look as if you wished the place in Hell,'
My friend said, 'judging from your face.' 'Oh well,
I suppose it's not the place's fault,' I said.

'Nothing, like something, happens anywhere.'

TIME'S FOOL

Time's fool, but not heaven's: yet hope not for
    any return.
The rabbit-eaten dry branch and the halfpenny
    candle
Are lost with the other treasure: the sooty kettle
Thrown away, become redbreast's home in the hedge,
    where the nettle
Shoots up, and bad bindweed wreathes rust-fretted
    handle.
Under that broken thing no more shall the dry
    branch burn.

Poor comfort all comfort: once what the mouse had
    spared
Was enough, was delight, there where the heart was
    at home;
The hard cankered apple holed by the wasp and
    the bird,
The damp bed, with the beetle's tap in the hardboard
    heard,
The dim bit of mirror, three inches of comb:
Dear enough, when with youth and with fancy
    shared.

I knew that the roots were creeping under the floor,
That the toad was safe in his hole, the poor cat by
      the fire,
The starling snug in the roof, each slept in his place:
The lily in splendour, the vine in her grace,
The fox in the forest, all had their desire,
As then I had mine, in the place that was happy
      and poor.

TOWN AND COUNTRY

The stately homes of England
How beautiful they stand!
Amidst their tall ancestral trees,
O'er all the pleasant land!

FELICIA HEMANS

I'm sitting pretty in a pretty little city.

FOX TROT SONG

From THE DESCRIPTION OF COOKE-HAM

Farewell (sweet *Cooke-ham*) where I first obtain'd
Grace from that Grace where perfit Grace remain'd;
And where the Muses gave their full consent,
I should have powre the virtuous to content:
Where princely Palace will'd me to indite,
The sacred Storie of the Soules delight.
Farewell (sweet Place) where Virtue then did rest,
And all delights did harbour in her breast:
Never shall my sad eies againe behold
Those pleasures which my thoughts did then unfold:
Yet you (great Lady) Mistris of that Place,
From whose desires did spring this worke of Grace;
Vouchsafe to thinke upon those pleasures past,
As fleeting worldly Joyes that could not last:
Or, as dimme shadowes of celestiall pleasures,
Which are desir'd above all earthly treasures.
Oh how (me thought) against you thither came,
Each part did seeme some new delight to frame!
The House receiv'd all ornaments to grace it,
And would indure no foulenesse to deface it.
The Walkes put on their summer Liveries,
And all things else did hold like similies:
The Trees with leaves, with fruits, with flowers clad,
Embrac'd each other, seeming to be glad,
Turning themselves to beauteous Canopies,
To shade the bright Sunne from your brighter eies:
The cristall Streames with silver spangles graced,

While by the glorious Sunne they were embraced:
The little Birds in chirping notes did sing,
To entertaine both You and that sweet Spring.
And *Philomela* with her sundry leyes,
Both You and that delightfull Place did praise.
Oh how me thought each plant, each floure, each tree
Set forth their beauties then to welcome thee.

AEMILIA LANYER (1569–1645)

MY GRANDMOTHER'S NEW YORK APARTMENT (I)

Everything pulled out or folded away:
sofa into a bed, tray tables that dis-
appear behind a door, everything
transmutable, alchemy in small
spaces, even my grandmother tiny
and changeable: a housecoat and rollers
which vanish and become an Irish
tweed suit, a tilted chapeau, a Hello
in the elevator just like, as she
would say, the Queen of Denmark.

EPODES, II

Happy the man who, free from business
    As Adam was when innocent,
Pretends to farm paternal acres
    And never thinks of the investment.

Nobody send him tiresome papers
    Which leave him utterly at sea;
He is not harried by his brokers
    Or people better off than he.

Oh no! He cultivates his vineyard
    And lets his vines get out of hand;
His cattle graze without regard
    To the condition of the land.

In pruning, he will always sever
    The fruiting branch, and leave the new;
At shearing, finds the sheep so clever
    He likes their wool best where it grew;

Finds honey sticky in the autumn
    And fruit a bit above his head;
He does not pick the pears, they all come
    Bouncing on top of him instead.

His wine is fit for a libation
    Upon the ground, but not to drink;
He much enjoys the preparation
    And he is proud if it is pink.

His private stream meanwhile runs purling,
    The birds sing as they're paid to do;
His fountains never tired of plashing
    And they are soporific too.

But when the proper sporting weather
    Arrives, he has to take a gun
And stir up something in the heather
    As gentlemen have always done,

Or even venture out on horse-back
    And hope a fox will come his way;
How awkward he should lose the pack
    So very early in the day!

With such delights he can forget
    That tiresome girl at the week-end:
He plans to have, but not just yet,
    A wife on whom he can depend

– Children perhaps – some sunburnt lady,
    He'd feel a proper farmer then;
She'd bring in firewood, have tea ready,
    He'd come in tired, not curious when

She penned the geese or milked the cows,
    So long as she'd drawn cider and,
From home-grown chicken and potatoes,
    Prepared a meal with her own hands.

No Yarmouth oysters could be sweeter,
　　Smoked salmon, turbot, what you please,
Not any delicacy caught here
　　Or found, long dead, in the deep freeze.

It's not too bad to dine off pheasant
　　But home-grown olives do as well,
And what he finds extremely pleasant
　　Is chewing meadow-sweet and sorrel:

Which one of course can supplement
　　By hedgerow herbs that taste of tar,
Or better, when such boons are sent
　　A lamb run over by a car.

'Amidst such treats as these, how fine
　　To see beasts by your own front door,
The latest plough, the latest combine,
　　And plan what you will use them for.'

So spoke the city man, and sold
　　The lot, preferring stocks and shares.
Too bad that he had not been told
　　The full extent of rural cares.

HORACE (65–8 BCE)
TR. C. H. SISSON

POSH

Where I live is posh
  Sundays the lawns are mown
My neighbours drink papaya squash

Sushi is a favourite nosh
  Each six-year-old has a mobile phone
Where I live is posh

In spring each garden is awash
  with wisteria, pink and fully blown
My neighbours drink papaya squash

Radicchio thrives beneath the cloche
  Cannabis is home grown
Where I live is posh

Appliances by Míele and Bosch
  Sugar-free jam on wholemeal scone
My neighbours drink papaya squash

Birds hum and bees drone
  The paedophile is left alone
My neighbours drink papaya squash
Where I live is posh.

SHITE

Where I live is shite
   An inner-city high-rise shack
Social workers shoot on sight

The hospital's been set alight
   The fire brigade's under attack
Where I live is shite

Police hide under their beds at night
   Every road's a cul-de-sac
Social workers shoot on sight

Girls get pregnant just for spite
   My mate's a repo-maniac
Where I live is shite.

Newborn junkies scratch and bite
   Six-year-olds swap sweets for crack
Social workers shoot on sight

Tattooed upon my granny's back
   A fading wrinkled Union Jack
Social workers shoot on sight
Where I live is shite.

ROGER McGOUGH (1937–)   191

CHORES

All day he's shoveled green pine sawdust
out of the trailer truck into the chute.
From time to time he's clambered down to even
the pile. Now his hair is frosted with sawdust.
Little rivers of sawdust pour out of his boots.

I hope in the afterlife there's none of this stuff
he says, stripping nude in the late September sun
while I broom off his jeans, his sweater flocked
with granules, his immersed-in-sawdust socks.
I hope there's no bedding, no stalls, no barn

no more repairs to the paddock gate the horses
burst through when snow avalanches off the roof.
Although the old broodmare, our first foal, is his,
horses, he's fond of saying, make divorces.
Fifty years married, he's safely facetious.

No garden pump that's airbound, no window a grouse
flies into and shatters, no ancient tractor's
intractable problem with carburetor
ignition or piston, no mowers and no chain saws
that refuse to start, or start, misfire and quit.

But after a Bloody Mary on the terrace
already frost-heaved despite our heroic efforts
to level the bricks a few years back, he says

let's walk up to the field and catch the sunset
and off we go, a couple of aging fools.

I hope, he says, on the other side there's a lot
less work, but just in case I'm bringing tools.

MAXINE KUMIN (1925–2014)

ECONOMICS

Everything comes down to numbers in the end.

This morning a blackbird woke me up; five swans
        in formation
trailed their silver chevrons upriver, unbothered by
the heron's slow torpedo; three horses in maroon
        jackets stood
mystified by their own breath. A greenfinch and
        thirty-nine
cows patterned the field; twin black labs trotted
        through
the long grass, jingling, and unearthed a compact
        of magpies.
I didn't count the dandelion clocks, there were
        so many.

You ask me would I move to the city to be with you.
I'm telling you what I saw; you can do the maths.

REBECCA WATTS (1983–)   193

FEET OFF THE GROUND

On the ground floor the wealthy and their cats
minded each other's business, but above
in the topmost branches of the flats
two, like their neighbours, lived on crusts and love.

Sparrow jazz shook them awake; pigeon hymns,
sacred on Sunday, all the week profane,
composed at nightfall their haphazard limbs.
And a crow made its pulpit in the drain.

If sometimes, towards evening, he let fall
out of his fingers' nest a clutch of words,
singing poured out of the window, and all
her birds were poems and all his poems birds.

THE PEOPLE
NEXT DOOR

Love your neighbour, yet pull not downe your hedge.

GEORGE HERBERT, *Outlandish Proverbs*

A QUIET NEIGHBOUR

Accounted our commodities,
Few more commodious reason sees
Than is this one commodity,
Quietly neighboured to be.
Which neighbourhood in thee appears.
For we two having ten whole years
Dwelt wall to wall, so joiningly,
That whispering soundeth through well-nigh,
I never heard thy servants brawl
More than thou hadst had none at all.
Nor I can no way make avaunt
That ever I heard thee give them taunt.
Thou art to them and they to thee
More mild than mute – mum ye be.
I hear no noise mine ease to break,
Thy butt'ry door I hear not creak.
Thy kitchen cumbreth not by heat,
Thy cooks chop neither herbs nor meat.
I never heard thy fire once spark,
I never heard thy dog once bark.
I never heard once in thy house
So much as one peep of one mouse.
I never heard thy cat once mew.
These praises are not small nor few.
I bear all water of thy soil,
Whereof I feel no filthy foil,
Save water which doth wash thy hands,

Wherein there none annoyance stands.
Of all thy guests set at thy board
I never heard one speak one word.
I never heard them cough nor hem.
I think thence to Jerusalem,
For this neighbourly quietness
Thou art the neighbour neighbourless.
For ere thou wouldst neighbour annoy
These kinds of quiet to destroy,
Thou rather wouldst to help that matter
At home alone fast bread and water.

JOHN HEYWOOD (*c.* 1497–*c.* 1580)

I, 86: MY NEIGHBOUR, NOVIUS

Novius is my neighbour, and can be touched by the hand from my windows. Who would not envy me, and think me every hour of the day happy in being able to enjoy so close a comrade? He is as far from me as Terentianus who now governs Syene on the Nile. I can't dine with him, nor even see him or hear him, and in all the city there is no man who is so near and yet so far from me. I must shift farther, or he must. You should be Novius's neighbour, or fellow-lodger, if you don't wish to see Novius.

MARTIAL (*c.* 40–*c.* 104)
TR. WALTER C. A. KER

NEIGHBOURS

From the bay windows
Of the mouldering hotel across the road from us
Mysterious, one-night itinerants emerge
On to their balconies
To breathe the cool night air.

We let them stare
In at our quiet lives.
They let us wonder what's become of them.

IAN HAMILTON (1938–2001)

NEIGHBOURS

I am the type you are supposed to fear
Black and foreign
Big and dreadlocks
An uneducated grass eater.

I talk in tongues
I chant at night
I appear anywhere,
I sleep with lions
And when the moon gets me
I am a Wailer.

I am moving in
Next door to you
So you can get to know me,
You will see my shadow
In the bathroom window,
My aromas will occupy
Your space,
Our ball will be in your court.
How will you feel?

You should feel good
You have been chosen.

I am the type you are supposed to love
Dark and mysterious
Tall and natural
Thinking, tea total.
I talk in schools
I sing on TV
I am in the papers,
I keep cool cats

And when the sun is shining
I go Carnival.

NEIGHBORS

They live alone
together,

she with her wide hind
and bird face,
he with his hung belly
and crewcut.

They never talk
but keep busy.

Today they are
washing windows
(each window together)
she on the inside,
he on the outside.
He squirts Windex
at her face,
she squirts Windex
at his face.

Now they are waving
to each other
with rags,

not smiling.

From WORKS AND DAYS (Book II)

Call your friend to a feast; but leave your enemy alone;
and especially call him who lives near you: for if any
mischief happen in the place, neighbours come ungirt,
but kinsmen stay to gird themselves. A bad neighbour
is as great a plague as a good one is a great blessing;
he who enjoys a good neighbour enjoys honour. Not
even an ox would die but for a bad neighbour. Take fair
measure from your neighbour and pay him back fairly
with the same measure, or better, if you can; so that
if you are in need afterwards, you may find him sure.

HESIOD (*fl.* 700 BCE)
TR. HUGH G. EVELYN-WHITE

BREEZEWAY

Someone said we needed a breezeway
to bark down remnants of super storm Elias jugularly.
Alas it wasn't my call.
I didn't have a call or anything resembling one.
You see I have always been a rather dull-spirited
        winch.
The days go by and I go with them.
A breeze falls from a nearby tower,
finds no breezeway, goes away
along a mission to supersize red shutters.

Alas if that were only all.
There's the children's belongings to be looked to
if only one can find the direction needed
and stuff like that.
I said we were all homers not homos
but my voice dwindled in the roar of Hurricane
        Edsel.
We have to live out our precise experimentation.
Otherwise there's no dying for anybody,
no crisp rewards.

Batman came out and clubbed me.
He never did get along with my view of the universe
except you know existential threads
from the time of the peace beaters and more.
He patted his dog Pastor Fido.
There was still so much to be learned
and even more to be researched.
It was like a goodbye. Why not accept it,
anyhow? The mission girls came through the woods
in their special suitings. It was all whipped cream
        and baklava.
Is there a Batman somewhere, who notices us
and promptly looks away, at a new catalog, say,
or another racing car expletive
coming back at Him?

MENDING WALL

Something there is that doesn't love a wall,
That sends the frozen-ground-swell under it,
And spills the upper boulders in the sun;
And makes gaps even two can pass abreast.
The work of hunters is another thing:
I have come after them and made repair
Where they have left not one stone on a stone,
But they would have the rabbit out of hiding,
To please the yelping dogs. The gaps I mean,
No one has seen them made or heard them made,
But at spring mending-time we find them there.
I let my neighbor know beyond the hill;
And on a day we meet to walk the line
And set the wall between us once again.
We keep the wall between us as we go.
To each the boulders that have fallen to each.
And some are loaves and some so nearly balls
We have to use a spell to make them balance:
'Stay where you are until our backs are turned!'
We wear our fingers rough with handling them.
Oh, just another kind of outdoor game,
One on a side. It comes to little more:
There where it is we do not need the wall:
He is all pine and I am apple orchard.
My apple trees will never get across
And eat the cones under his pines, I tell him
He only says, 'Good fences make good neighbors.'

Spring is the mischief in me, and I wonder
If I could put a notion in his head:
'*Why* do they make good neighbors? Isn't it
Where there are cows? But here there are no cows.
Before I built a wall I'd ask to know
What I was walling in or walling out,
And to whom I was like to give offense.
Something there is that doesn't love a wall,
That wants it down.' I could say 'Elves' to him,
But it's not elves exactly, and I'd rather
He said it for himself. I see him there
Bringing a stone grasped firmly by the top
In each hand, like an old-stone savage armed.
He moves in darkness as it seems to me,
Not of woods only and the shade of trees
He will not go behind his father's saying,
And he likes having thought of it so well
He says again, 'Good fences make good neighbors.'

THE NOD

Saturday evenings we would stand in line
In Loudan's butcher shop. Red beef, white string,
Brown paper ripped straight off for parcelling
Along the counter edge. Rib roast and shin
Plonked down, wrapped up, and bow-tied neat
    and clean
But seeping blood. Like dead weight in a sling,
Heavier far than I had been expecting
While my father shelled out for it, coin by coin.

Saturday evenings too the local B-Men,
Unbuttoned but on duty, thronged the town,
Neighbours with guns, parading up and down,
Some nodding at my father almost past him
As if deliberately they'd aimed and missed him
Or couldn't seem to place him, not just then.

ENTERTAINING

home is the resort
Of love, of joy, of peace, and plenty, where,
Supporting and supported, polish'd friends,
And dear relations mingle into bliss.

JAMES THOMSON

CEREMONIES FOR CHRISTMASSE

Come, bring with a noise,
My merrie merrie boyes,
The Christmas log to the firing;
While my good dame, she
Bids ye all be free,
And drink to your hearts desiring.

With the last yeeres brand
Light the new block, and
For good successe in his spending,
On your psaltries play,
That sweet luck may
Come while the log is a teending.

Drink now the strong beere,
Cut the white loafe here,
The while the meat is a shredding;
For the rare mince-pie,
And the plums stand by,
To fill the paste that's a kneading.

ROBERT HERRICK (1591–1674)   209

DINING-ROOM TEA

When you were there, and you, and you,
Happiness crowned the night; I too,
Laughing and looking, one of all,
I watched the quivering lamplight fall
On plate and flowers and pouring tea
And cup and cloth; and they and we
Flung all the dancing moments by
With jest and glitter. Lip and eye
Flashed on the glory, shone and cried,
Improvident, unmemoried;
And fitfully and like a flame
The light of laughter went and came.
Proud in their careless transience moved
The changing faces that I loved.

Till suddenly, and otherwhence,
I looked upon your innocence.
For lifted clear and still and strange
From the dark woven flow of change
Under a vast and starless sky
I saw the immortal moment lie.
One instant I, an instant, knew
As God knows all. And it and you
I, above Time, oh, blind! could see
In witless immortality.

I saw the marble cup; the tea,
Hung on the air, an amber stream;
I saw the fire's unglittering gleam,
The painted flame, the frozen smoke.
No more the flooding lamplight broke
On flying eyes and lips and hair;
But lay, but slept unbroken there,
On stiller flesh, and body breathless,
And lips and laughter stayed and deathless,
And words on which no silence grew.
Light was more alive than you.

For suddenly, and otherwhence,
I looked on your magnificence.
I saw the stillness and the light,
And you, august, immortal, white,
Holy and strange; and every glint
Posture and jest and thought and tint
Freed from the mask of transiency,
Triumphant in eternity,
Immote, immortal.

      Dazed at length
Human eyes grew, mortal strength
Wearied; and Time began to creep.
Change closed about me like a sleep.
Light glinted on the eyes I loved.
The cup was filled. The bodies moved.
The drifting petal came to ground.
The laughter chimed its perfect round.

The broken syllable was ended.
And I, so certain and so friended,
How could I cloud, or how distress,
The heaven of your unconsciousness?
Or shake at Time's sufficient spell,
Stammering of lights unutterable?
The eternal holiness of you,
The timeless end, you never knew,
The peace that lay, the light that shone.
You never knew that I had gone
A million miles away, and stayed
A million years. The laughter played
Unbroken round me; and the jest
Flashed on. And we that knew the best
Down wonderful hours grew happier yet.
I sang at heart, and talked, and eat,
And lived from laugh to laugh, I too,
When you were there, and you, and you.

HOW TO GET ON IN SOCIETY

Phone for the fish-knives, Norman
    As Cook is a little unnerved,
You kiddies have crumpled the serviettes
    And I must have things daintily served.

Are the requisites all in the toilet?
    The frills round the cutlets can wait
Till the girl has replenished the cruets
    And switched on the logs in the grate.

It's ever so close in the lounge, dear,
    But the vestibule's comfy for tea
And Howard is out riding on horseback
    So do come and take some with me.

Now here is a fork for your pastries
    And do use the couch for your feet;
I know what I wanted to ask you –
    Is trifle sufficient for sweet?

Milk and then just as it comes dear?
    I'm afraid the preserve's full of stones;
Beg pardon, I'm soiling the doilies
    With afternoon tea-cakes and scones.

CHILDREN'S PARTY

May I join you in the doghouse, Rover?
I wish to retire till the party's over.
Since three o'clock I've done my best
To entertain each tiny guest;
My conscience now I've left behind me,
And if they want me, let them find me.
I blew their bubbles, I sailed their boats,
I kept them from each other's throats,
I told them tales of magic lands,
I took them out to wash their hands.
I sorted their rubbers and tied their laces,
I wiped their noses and dried their faces.
Of similarity there's lots
Twixt tiny tots and Hottentots.
I've earned repose to heal the ravages
Of these angelic-looking savages.
Oh, progeny playing by itself
Is a lonely fascinating elf,
But progeny in roistering batches
Would drive St. Francis from here to Natchez.
Shunned are the games a parent proposes;
They prefer to squirt each other with hoses,
Their playmates are their natural foemen
And they like to poke each other's abdomen.
Their joy needs another's woe to cushion it,
Say a puddle, and somebody littler to push in it.

They observe with glee the ballistic results
Of ice cream with spoons for catapults,
And inform the assembly with tears and glares
That everyone's presents are better than theirs.
Oh, little women and little men,
Someday I hope to love you again,
But not till after the party's over,
So give me the key to the doghouse, Rover.

OGDEN NASH (1902–71)

GETTING IT BACK

When the guests have gone, the house is twice
as big. Quiet blows through it like silver
light that touches every chair and plate
to the precision of objects in a Vermeer.

We face each other and slowly begin to talk,
not making conversation as one plans and then
cooks a company dinner, but improvising,
the words spiraling up and out in a dance

as intricate and instinctual as the choral
wave of swallows darting on the silken
twilight pale as a moon snail shell, till between
us the hanging nest of our intimacy is rewoven.

MARGE PIERCY (1936–)   215

SILENCE

My father used to say,
'Superior people never make long visits,
have to be shown Longfellow's grave
or the glass flowers at Harvard.
Self-reliant like the cat –
that takes its prey to privacy,
the mouse's limp tail hanging like a shoelace from
      its mouth –
they sometimes enjoy solitude,
and can be robbed of speech
by speech which has delighted them.
The deepest feeling always shows itself in silence;
not in silence, but restraint.'
Nor was he insincere in saying, 'Make my house
      your inn.'
Inns are not residences.

MARIANNE MOORE (1887–1972)

III, 27: DINNER INVITATIONS

Though I invite you, Gallus, you never invite me back:
I'd forgive you, Gallus, if you never invited a soul.
You do, though: we both have faults. 'Which?' you ask,
I've no sense, Gallus, and you've no shame.

MARTIAL (*c.* 40–*c.* 104)
TR. A. S. KLINE

plum blossom scent –
for whoever shows up
a cracked teacup

ISSA (1763–1828)
TR. DAVID G. LANOUE

VISITOR

I am dreaming of a house just like this one

but larger and opener to the trees, nighter

than day and higher than noon, and you,

visiting, knocking to get in, hoping for icy

milk or hot tea or whatever it is you like.

For each night is a long drink in a short glass.

A drink of blacksound water, such a rush

and fall of lonesome no form can contain it.

And if it isn't night yet, though I seem to

recall that it is, then it is not for everyone.

Did you receive my invitation? It is not

for everyone. Please come to my house

lit by leaf light. It's like a book with bright

pages filled with flocks and glens and groves
and overlooked by Pan, that seductive satyr
in whom the fish is also cooked. A book that
took too long to read but minutes to unread –
that is – to forget. Strange are the pages
thus. Nothing but the hope of company.
I made too much pie in expectation. I was
hoping to sit with you in a treehouse in a
nightgown in a real way. Did you receive
my invitation? Written in haste, before
leaf blinked out, before the idea fully formed.
An idea like a stormcloud that does not spill
or arrive but moves silently in a direction.
Like a dark book in a long life with a vague
hope in a wood house with an open door.

DECEPTIVELY
SPACIOUS

A grass-thatched hut
    less than five feet square:
regrettable indeed
    to build even this –
if only there were no rains

BUTCHO

'SMALL HOUSE AND QUIET ROOF TREE'

Small house and quiet roof tree, shadowing elm,
Grapes on the vine and cherries ripening,
Red apples in the orchard, Pallas' tree
Breaking with olives, and well-watered earth,
And fields of kale and heavy creeping mallows
And poppies that will surely bring me sleep.
And if I go a-snaring for the birds
Or timid deer, or angling the shy trout,
'Tis all the guile that my poor fields will know.
Go now, yea, go, and sell your life, swift life,
For golden feasts. If the end waits me too,
I pray it find me here, and here shall ask
The reckoning from me of the vanished hours.

PETRONIUS ARBITER (c. 27 – 66)
TR. HELEN WADDELL

THE LAKE ISLE OF INNISFREE

I will arise and go now, and go to Innisfree,
And a small cabin build there, of clay and
      wattles made:
Nine bean-rows will I have there, a hive for
      the honey-bee,
And live alone in the bee-loud glade.

And I shall have some peace there, for peace comes
      dropping slow,
Dropping from the veils of the morning to where the
      cricket sings;
There midnight's all a glimmer, and noon a
      purple glow,
And evening full of the linnet's wings.

I will arise and go now, for always night and day
I hear lake water lapping with low sounds by
      the shore;
While I stand on the roadway, or on the
      pavements grey,
I hear it in the deep heart's core.

INSIDE MY ZULU HUT

It is a hive
without any bees
to build the walls
with golden bricks of honey.
A cave cluttered
with a millstone,
calabashes of sour milk
claypots of foaming beer
sleeping grass mats
wooden head rests
tanned goat skins
tied with *riempies*
to wattle rafters
blackened by the smoke
of kneaded cow dung
burning under
the three-legged pot
on the earthen floor
to cook my porridge.

From THE TASK

Peace to the artist, whose ingenious thought
Devised the weather-house, that useful toy!
Fearless of humid air and gathering rains
Forth steps the man, an emblem of myself,
More delicate his tim'rous mate retires.
When Winter soaks the fields, and female feet
Too weak to struggle with tenacious clay,
Or ford the rivulets, are best at home,
The task of new discov'ries falls on me.
At such a season and with such a charge
Once went I forth, and found, till then unknown,
A cottage, whither oft we since repair:
'Tis perch'd upon the green-hill top, but close
Inviron'd with a ring of branching elms
That overhang the thatch, itself unseen,
Peeps at the vale below; so thick beset
With foliage of such dark redundant growth,
I call'd the low-roof'd lodge the *peasant's nest.*
And hidden as it is, and far remote
From such unpleasing sounds as haunt the ear
In village or in town, the bay of curs
Incessant, clinking hammers, grinding wheels,
And infants clam'rous whether pleas'd or pain'd,
Oft have I wish'd the peaceful covert mine.
Here, I have said, at least I should possess
The poet's treasure, silence, and indulge
The dreams of fancy, tranquil and secure.

Vain thought! the dweller in that still retreat
Dearly obtains the refuge it affords.
Its elevated scite forbids the wretch
To drink sweet waters of the chrystal well;
He dips his bowl into the weedy ditch,
And heavy-laden brings his bev'rage home
Far-fetch'd and little worth; nor seldom waits,
Dependent on the baker's punctual call,
To hear his creaking panniers at the door,
Angry and sad and his last crust consumed.
So farewel envy of the *peasant's nest.*
If solitude make scant the means of life,
Society for me! Thou seeming sweet,
Be still a pleasing object in my view,
My visit still, but never mine abode.

THE HOUSE OF SOCRATES

For *Socrates* a House was built,
    Of but inferior Size;
Not highly Arch'd, nor Carv'd, nor Gilt;
    The Man, 'tis said, was Wise.

But *Mob* despis'd the little Cell,
    That struck them with no Fear;
Whilst Others thought, there should not dwell
    So great a Person there.

How shou'd a due Recourse be made
    To One, so much Admir'd?
Where shou'd the spacious Cloth be laid,
    Or where the Guests retir'd?

Believe me, quoth the list'ning Sage,
    'Twas not to save the Charge;
That in this over-building Age,
    My House was not more large.

But this for faithful Friends, and kind,
    Was only meant by me;
Who fear that what too streight you find,
    Must yet contracted be.

SMALL HOUSE

Small house, but throw a ball through it some time
and it becomes quite large. See all those metres,
aren't they ours? And stroll perhaps as if
you don't know where you're going: space is
stretching out and yawns between the walls. Behold:
the wandering that binds the rooms together
has been painted white. There are some stairs,
a hat stand in the cupboard, doors. As if
by accident it lies there like a country
lane, where roads determine goal and starting
point and not the other way around. If you
go out for bread and then return you'll see
that we can organise a picnic. Quick!
Go now! The shrinking can't be far away.

MARK BOOG (1970–)
TR. WILLEN GROENEWEGEN

THE BLUE-EYED GIANT,
THE MINIATURE WOMAN AND
THE HONEYSUCKLE

He was a blue-eyed giant,
he loved a miniature woman.
The woman's dream was of a miniature house
    with a garden where honeysuckle grows
     in a riot of colours
      that sort of house.

The giant loved like a giant,
and his hands were used to such big things
    that the giant could not
make the building,
    could not knock on the door
of the garden where the honeysuckle grows
    in a riot of colours
      at that house.

He was a blue-eyed giant,
he loved a miniature woman,
a mini miniature woman.
The woman was hungry for comfort
    and tired of the giant's long strides.
And bye bye off she went to the embraces of a
      rich dwarf
    with a garden where the honeysuckle grows
    in a riot of colours
     that sort of house.

Now the blue-eyed giant realizes,
there can't even be a grave for giant loves:
in the garden where honeysuckle grows
    in a riot of colours
        that sort of house . . .

NAZIM HIKMET (1902–63)
TR. RICHARD McKANE

My hut lies in the middle of a dense forest;
Every year the green ivy grows longer.
No news of the affairs of men,
Only the occasional song of a woodcutter.
The sun shines and I mend my robe;
When the moon comes out I read Buddhist poems.
I have nothing to report, my friends.
If you want to find the meaning, stop chasing after
        so many things.

RYOKAN (1758–1831)
TR. JOHN STEVENS

This little house
No smaller than the world
Nor I lonely
Dwelling in all that is.

SAFE AS HOUSES

Ladybird, ladybird fly away home,
Your house is on fire and your children all gone ...

TRAD.

For a man's house is his castle.

EDWARD COKE

MY HOUSE

My house
Is granite
It fronts
North,

Where the Firth flows,
East the sea.
My room
holds the first

Blow from the North,
The first from East,
Salt upon
The pane.

In the dark
I, a child,
Did not know
The consuming night

And heard
The wind,
Unworried and
Warm – secure.

BLOCK CITY

What are you able to build with your blocks?
Castles and palaces, temples and docks.
Rain may keep raining, and others go roam,
But I can be happy and building at home.

Let the sofa be mountains, the carpet be sea,
There I'll establish a city for me:
A kirk and a mill and a palace beside,
And a harbour as well where my vessels may ride.

Great is the palace with pillar and wall,
A sort of a tower on the top of it all,
And steps coming down in an orderly way
To where my toy vessels lie safe in the bay.

This one is sailing and that one is moored:
Hark to the song of the sailors on board!
And see on the steps of my palace, the kings
Coming and going with presents and things!

Now I have done with it, down let it go!
All in a moment the town is laid low.
Block upon block lying scattered and free,
What is there left of my town by the sea?

Yet as I saw it, I see it again,
The kirk and the palace, the ships and the men,
And as long as I live, and where'er I may be,
I'll always remember my town by the sea.

THE PLAYHOUSE

We little girls
make the outer walls
of our playhouse
with pearls from golden conches
    which surround the fragrant golden water.

We make our cooking pots
from right-whirling conches.

We fill the pots with rich honey,
    produced when buds break
    in the seed pods of red lotuses
    growing in newly-planted fields.

We cook our rice,
    made of pearls from bamboos.

We make our curry
from freshly picked bunches of flowers
grown in a grove
as fragrant as rosewater.

See how eagerly we cook
our precious rice.

Don't destroy our playhouse,
with your fair young feet,
redolent from the head of Indra.

Don't destroy our playhouse,
rich one of Tiruccentūr,
where waves wash up pearls.

PAKAḺIKKŪTTAṈ (c. 1375–1425)
TR. PAULA S. RICHMAN

HEARTHSTONE

Lifting the slab takes our breath away
Corner to edge, edge to corner.
Its weight steps the plank
shifting from foot to foot.

The van groans slowly home.
We pause to think, eye the gap
and heave again.
A quarter of a ton.

What weighs is the power of it
trembling at finger-tip,
its balancing moment
held like feathers.

Grindings pressed to slate
electric in my hands. We lean
on the ropes and let it
slowly into fresh cement.

Its purples multiplied
as snows, rains, rivers
that laid themselves down
too finely to see or count,

as many stone-years as wings
of the heath blue, jay feather, layers
of oak-shadow, beechmast,
print of a mountain-ash on rockface.

The tree in the crevice, quarryman
in the glittering slip of rain
on million-faceted blue Blaenau,
the purples of Penrhyn.

So the dairy slab that cooled
junkets and wheys, wide dishes of milk
beading with cream, skims for churning,
now becomes pentanfaen,

hearthstone. Milky planets
trapped in its sheets
when the book was printed,
float in the slate,

water-marked pages
under a stove's feet.

VERSES UPON THE BURNING OF OUR HOUSE, JULY 10TH, 1666

In silent night when rest I took,
For sorrow neer I did not look,
I waken'd was with thundring nois
And piteous shreiks of dreadfull voice.
That fearfull sound of fire and fire,
Let no man know is my Desire.
I starting up the light did spye,
And to my God my heart did cry
To strengthen me in my Distresse
And not to leave me succourlesse.
Then coming out beheld a space
The flame consume my dwelling place.
And when I could no longer look
I blest his Name that gave and took,
That layd my goods now in the dust
Yea so it was, and so 'twas just.
It was his own it was not mine
Far be it that I should repine,
He might of All justly bereft,
But yet sufficient for us left.
When by the Ruines oft I past
My sorrowing eyes aside did cast
And here and there the places spye
Where oft I sate and long did lye,
Here stood that Trunk, and there that chest,
There lay that store I counted best

My pleasant things in ashes lye
And them behold no more shall I.
Under thy roof no guest shall sitt,
Nor at thy Table eat a bitt.
No pleasant tale shall 'ere be told
Nor things recounted done of old.
No Candle 'ere shall shine in Thee,
Nor bridegroom's voice ere heard shall bee.
In silence ever shalt thou lye
Adeiu, Adeiu, All's Vanity.
Then streight I 'gin my heart to chide,
And did thy wealth on earth abide,
Didst fix thy hope on mouldring dust,
The arm of flesh didst make thy trust?
Raise up thy thoughts above the skye
That dunghill mists away may flie.
Thou hast an house on high erect
Fram'd by that mighty Architect,
With glory richly furnished
Stands permanent tho: this bee fled.
'Its purchasèd and paid for too
By him who hath Enough to doe.
A prise so vast as is unknown
Yet by his Gift is made thine own.
Ther's wealth enough I need no more,
Farewell my pelf, farewell my Store.
The world no longer let me Love
My hope, and Treasure lyes Above.

a subtle matter

a house is burning

it looks like

there might be a house burning over there

like over there

there's a house burning

and so

and what

does this tell us

what it tells us

a good house

burns well

VSEVELOD NEKRASOV (1934–2009)
240   TR. AINSLEY MORSE AND BELA SHAYEVICH

SIRENSONG
(*for David*)

'What song the Syrens sang . . .'
SIR THOMAS BROWNE, *Urne Buriall*

I know the song they sang. I heard it,
The husky warbling, on the war's first day.
I learned the meaning, too: *Lie low, lie low.*

Gipsy women came to the door for help
With ration books they couldn't read. They gave us
Spuds from giant baskets; told no fortunes

(All fortunes were the same). Endlessly Mother
Explained about The Will, and who
Would take us on, if anything . . .

Ours had been a safe house. Safe as houses
Ever are. Built in a post-war country
It stood up straight, untroubled by rumours of war.

My baby knees crawled through it, certain of
          polished parquet,
Turkey carpets, quarry-tiled kitchen floor.
My knees understood this was a forever house.

The end of faith in brick. The house fluttered,
As trespassing aircraft droned life-long overhead,
Leaving the town rubble and honeycomb.

We were precocious experts on shrapnel and blast.
Things broken weren't replaced. What was the point?
Friends were lost, too. You didn't talk of it.

We knew how bombs sliced off a house's flank,
Uncovering private parts; how bedroom grates
Still stuck to walls though wallpaper flailed outside;

How baths slewed rudely, rakishly into view;
How people noted, and talked of what they saw;
How ours might be the next; and what they'd say.

Peace made no difference. Still too young to matter,
Someone still fighting somewhere, some children
Are invaded for ever, will never learn to be young.

We missed the jazz and swing of our extrovert
       parents,
The pyrotechnic raves of our groovy kids.
Our ground was never steady underfoot.

We had no wax to cancel the sirens' song:
Lie low, lie low.

PLACE OF REFUGE

An oar lies on the roof. A moderate wind
Will not carry away the thatch.
In the yard posts are set for
The children's swing.
The mail comes twice a day
Where letters would be welcome.
Down the Sound come the ferries.
The house has four doors to escape by.

BERTOLT BRECHT (1898–1956)
TR. JOHN WILLETT

SAFE HOUSES

I find that I have started recently
to keep spare keys to the front door
in several pockets, such is my fear
of being locked out. Caught by the wind
the door could shut quietly behind you,
leaving you to face the outer world alone.
Once safe inside I don't put on the chain.

In guerrilla conflicts, the combatants
change their safe house at intervals
to give their hosts a rest from listening
for the thump on the door in the early hours,

as at the end of winter you escape
from cold and dark by making for
the sunnier climates to the south.

But where do we retreat to in the end
when the call to open up will not subside?
Kate in her nineties was no longer fit
to mind herself, so they took her in
to the Lee Road. When I called to see her
the nurse unlocked the door to the main room
and turned the key again behind me.

She was there with twenty other women,
all chattering and laughing like the magpies
in *Purgatorio*, not to each other
but to the unhearing outside world.
I thought of Masaccio's grieving couple,
not grasping what they've been exiled from,
some corner where the serpent cannot reach.

THE WITCH

I have walked a great while over the snow,
And I am not tall nor strong.
My clothes are wet, and my teeth are set,
And the way was hard and long.
I have wandered over the fruitful earth,
But I never came here before.
Oh, lift me over the threshold, and let me in at
     the door!

The cutting wind is a cruel foe.
I dare not stand in the blast.
My hands are stone, and my voice a groan,
And the worst of death is past.
I am but a little maiden still,
My little white feet are sore.
Oh, lift me over the threshold, and let me in at
     the door!

Her voice was the voice that women have,
Who plead for their heart's desire.
She came – she came – and the quivering flame
Sank and died in the fire.
It never was lit again on my hearth
Since I hurried across the floor,
To lift her over the threshold, and let her in at
     the door.

MARY E. COLERIDGE (1861–1907)

THE BROKEN PANE

It all conspires against you. Nasty weather,
lights that keep going out, and the old house
jolted by every gust. It's dear to you
for what you suffered in it, for the hopes
dashed there, and for a few good times as well.
Survival seems to you a refusal to obey
the way of things.
                         And in the shattering
of a window pane, you hear a judgment passed.

UMBERTO SABA (1883–1957)
TR. GEOFFREY BROCK

HOMELESS

And homeless near a thousand homes I stood,
And near a thousand tables pined, and wanted food.

WILLIAM WORDSWORTH

When you sit happy in your own fair house,
Remember all poor men that are abroad,
That Christ, who gave this roof, prepare for thee
Eternal dwelling in the house of God.

ALCUIN

'A LONELY WANDERER UPON EARTH AM I'

A lonely wanderer upon earth am I,
The waif of nature – like uprooted weed
Borne by the stream, or like a shaken reed,
A frail dependent of the fickle sky.
Far, far away, are all my natural kin:
The mother that erewhile hath hush'd my cry,
Almost hath grown a mere fond memory.
Where is my sister's smile? my brother's
     boisterous din?
Ah! nowhere now. A matron grave and sage,
A holy mother is that sister sweet.
And that bold brother is a pastor meet
To guide, instruct, reprove a sinful age,
Almost I fear, and yet I fain would greet;
So far astray hath been my pilgrimage.

HARTLEY COLERIDGE (1796–1849)

AN OLD WOMAN OF THE ROADS

O, to have a little house!
To own the hearth and stool and all!
The heaped up sods upon the fire,
The pile of turf against the wall!

To have a clock with weights and chains
And pendulum swinging up and down!
A dresser filled with shining delph,
Speckled and white and blue and brown!

I could be busy all the day
Clearing and sweeping hearth and floor,
And fixing on their shelf again
My white and blue and speckled store!

I could be quiet there at night
Beside the fire and by myself,
Sure of a bed and loth to leave
The ticking clock and the shining delph!

Och! but I'm weary of mist and dark,
And roads where there's never a house nor bush,
And tired I am of bog and road,
And the crying wind and the lonesome hush!

And I am praying to God on high,
And I am praying Him night and day,
For a little house – a house of my own –
Out of the wind's and the rain's way.

From THE VILLAGE

Theirs is yon house that holds the parish poor,
Whose walls of mud scarce bear the broken door;
There, where the putrid vapours, flagging, play,
And the dull wheel hums doleful through the day –
There children dwell, who know no parents' care;
Parents, who know no children's love, dwell there!
Heart-broken matrons on their joyless bed,
Forsaken wives, and mothers never wed;
Dejected widows with unheeded tears,
And crippled age with more than childhood fears;
The lame, the blind, and, far the happiest they!
The moping idiot and the madman gay.
Here too the sick their final doom receive,
Here brought, amid the scenes of grief, to grieve,
Where the loud groans from some sad chamber flow,
Mix'd with the clamours of the crowd below;
Here, sorrowing, they each kindred sorrow scan,
And the cold charities of man to man . . .

LIVING SPACE

There are just not enough
straight lines. That
is the problem.
Nothing is flat
or parallel. Beams
balance crookedly on supports
thrust off the vertical.
Nails clutch at open seams.
The whole structure leans dangerously
towards the miraculous.

Into this rough frame,
someone has squeezed
a living space

and even dared to place
these eggs in a wire basket,
fragile curves of white
hung out over the dark edge
of a slanted universe,
gathering the light
into themselves,
as if they were
the bright, thin walls of faith.

DREAM HOUSE

Safe upon the solid rock the ugly houses stand:
Come and see my shining palace built upon the sand!

EDNA ST. VINCENT MILLAY

ON LOSING A HOUSE

The bumble bees
know where their home is.
They have memorized
every stalk and leaf
of the field.
They fall from the air at
exactly
the right place,
they crawl
under the soft grasses,
they enter
the darkness
humming.

Where will we go
with our table and chairs,
our bed,
our nine thousand books,
our TV, PC, VCR,
our cat
who is sixteen years old?
Where will we put down
our dishes and our blue carpets,
where will we put up
our rose-colored,
rice-paper
shades?

We never saw
such a beautiful house,
though it dipped toward the sea,
though it shook and creaked,
though it said to the rain: come in!
and had a ghost –
at night she rattled the teacups
with her narrow hands,
then left the cupboard open –
and once she slipped – or maybe it wasn't a slip –
and called to our cat, who ran to the empty room.
We only smiled.
Unwise! Unwise!

O, what is money?
O, never in our lives have we thought
about money.
O, we have only a little money.
O, now in our sleep
we dream of finding money.
But someone else
already has money.
Money, money, money.
Someone else
can sign the papers,
can turn the key.
O dark, O heavy, O mossy money.

Amazing
how the rich
don't even
hesitate – up go the
sloping rooflines, out goes the
garden, down goes the crooked,
green tree, out goes the
old sink, and the little windows, and
there you have it – a house
like any other – and there goes
the ghost, and then another, they glide over
the water, away, waving and waving
their fog-colored hands.

Don't tell us
how to love, don't tell us
how to grieve, or what
to grieve for, or how loss
shouldn't sit down like a gray
bundle of dust in the deepest
pockets of our energy, don't laugh at our belief
that money isn't
everything, don't tell us
how to behave in
anger, in longing, in loss, in home-
sickness, don't tell us,
dear friends.

Goodbye, house.
Goodbye, sweet and beautiful house,
we shouted, and it shouted back,
goodbye to you, and lifted itself
down from the town, and set off
like a packet of clouds across
the harbor's blue ring,
the tossing bell, the sandy point – and turned
lightly, wordlessly,
into the keep of the wind
where it floats still –
where it plunges and rises still
on the black and dreamy sea.

THE WRONG HOUSE

I went into a house, and it wasn't a house,
    It has big steps and a great big hall;
But it hasn't got a garden,
        A garden,
        A garden,
    It isn't like a house at all.

I went into a house, and it wasn't a house,
    It has a big garden and great high wall;
But it hasn't got a may-tree,
        A may-tree,
        A may-tree,
    It isn't like a house at all.

I went into a house and it wasn't a house –
    Slow white petals from the may-tree fall;
But it hasn't got a blackbird,
        A blackbird,
        A blackbird,
    It isn't like a house at all.

I went into a house, and I thought it was a house,
    I could hear from the may-tree the blackbird
        call. . . .
But nobody listened to it,
        Nobody
        Liked it,
    Nobody wanted it at all.

A. A. MILNE (1882–1956)   259

THE OLD HOUSE

In through the porch and up the silent stair;
    Little is changed, I know so well the ways; –
Here, the dead came to meet me; it was there
    The dream was dreamed in unforgotten days.

But who is this that hurries on before,
    A flitting shade the brooding shades among? –
She turned, – I saw her face, – O God, it wore
    The face I used to wear when I was young!

I thought my spirit and my heart were tamed
    To deadness; dead the pangs that agonise.
The old grief springs to choke me, – I am shamed
    Before that little ghost with eager eyes.

O turn away, let her not see, not know!
    How should she bear it, how should understand?
O hasten down the stairway, haste and go,
    And leave her dreaming in the silent land.

THE PAST

Let no one say the past is dead.
The past is all about us and within.
Haunted by tribal memories, I know
This little now, this accidental present
Is not the all of me, whose long making
Is so much of the past.

Tonight here in suburbia as I sit
In easy chair before electric heater,
Warmed by the red glow, I fall into dream:
I am away
At the camp fire in the bush, among
My own people, sitting on the ground,
No walls about me,
The stars over me,
The tall surrounding trees that stir in the wind
Making their own music,
Soft cries of the night coming to us, there
Where we are one with all old Nature's lives
Known and unknown,
In scenes where we belong but have now forsaken.
Deep chair and electric radiator
Are but since yesterday,

But a thousand thousand camp fires in the forest
Are in my blood.
Let none tell me the past is wholly gone.
Now is so small a part of time, so small a part
Of all the race years that have moulded me.

OODGEROO NOONUCCAL (1920–93)   261

'HERE IS AN ISLAND . . .'

Here is an island. Here is a house on stilts.
A black log house,
With a window open wide.
Green waves wash up to it,
But no one lives inside,
Not for many years.
Only I live here,
Drying seaweed
To cook for meals,
And I have lived for thousands of years.
But where I used to live,
Where they used to love me
They think that I have died,
They mourned and then forgot me.
But I live on and on . . .
Under the thundering green,
I call my friends to meals
On a voiceless telephone.

BELLA DIZHUR (1903–2006)
262   TR. SARAH W. BLIUMIS

THE ESTATE AGENT'S DAUGHTER

is sold as seen,
semi-detached,
in walking distance of Pen-
y-Bont ar Ogwr with all its mod cons,
located in a quiet hammerhead.

She has wrought iron gates,
hard standing parking for two.
Her pea gravel driveway sweeps
to a Cloudy Apple composite door,
stained window with leaded detail.

Her hallway is carpeted with sycamore
seeds and cherry blossom throughout.
Her white dogleg staircase leads to a spindle
gallery landing, with access to a loft
conversion with a skylight window.

Ground floor comprises open plan lounge/diner,
recesses either side of fire breast wall.
Her writing desk has been nudged to the brink
of the bay. Curtains may be drawn
around her to quarantine at will.

Dining table moonlights as tributary desk,
cable-knit cardigans draped across Ikea
chairs come as standard.
Spider-warding conkers mob
her laminated corners in vain.

She boasts a galley kitchen
with splashback tiling. Integrated
fridge/freezer, sunken spotlighting,
eye level oven (rarely used)
white goods to remain.

The master bedroom is in need of updating,
juliet balcony in state of disrepair.
Outside: She has a storm porch
with power and lighting,
chipped area to the side.

The estate agent's daughter retains
many original features, coved
ceilings, double glazing throughout.
Unsuitable for first time buyers,
no ongoing chain.

ON HOUSES AND HOMES: MEDITATIONS

Old houses were scaffolding once
and workmen whistling.

T. E. HULME

Your house shall not be an anchor but a mast . . .
And though of magnificence and splendour, your house shall not hold your secret nor shelter your longing.
For that which is boundless in you abides in the mansion of the sky, whose door is the morning mist, and whose windows are the songs and silences of night.

KAHLIL GIBRAN

A HOUSE WE CAN NEVER FIND

We couldn't wait
to leave their house,
to lie with lovers whose names
are forgotten now, to take risks
with our minds and bodies,
to live in countries
that never asked to have us,
or thanked us afterwards,
racing through the years with rage,
towards something that we
finally have one day,
and which is no more, no less
than the certainty of not
hearing their steps
creaking, measuring the floorboards
of a house we can never find.

WHAT WE KNOW OF HOUSES
From *Settlements*

God answers our prayers by refusing them.
                              LUTHER

Sunday
          We are driving to the woods
to find the hidden origin of rain:
a shallow basin carved into the rock
where Pictish chiefs assembled with their kin
to reinvent the world
                    – or so we say –
though no one knows for sure who gathered here
or why.

          I like to think of them
on days like this
perched on a shelf of rock beneath the trees
watching their children
                        thinking of their stock
then stepping out
              to sacrifice
                        or blessing
as we have stood together in the shade
made awkward by the quiet of the place
a darkness that continues while the sun
brightens the fields

                    and gardens fill with light
in market towns or tidy golf-hotels
above the sea.

Though nothing here is sacred
                                – not to us –
even the pool of water stopped with leaves
the carvings in the rock
                        the standing stone
are set apart

and nothing we can touch or say will bring us
closer to the spirit of the place.
Our holy ground is barely recognised:
unverified
            an atmospheric trick
a common miracle that finds us out
alone in attic rooms
                    as spring begins:
a rhythm in the light
                    a line of song
the sudden taste of grass
                            high in the roof
wind through the gaps in the beams
                            the rafters spiced
with cumin
and the aftertaste of nets

and all along the roads
                        where dry-stone walls
have toppled
            and the steady gorse digs in
embers of perfume, sealed in a crown of thorns:

unseasonable   stubborn   everyday
– it's bright as the notion of home:
                              not something held
or given
        but the painful gravity
that comes of being settled on the earth
redeemable   inventive   inexact
and capable of holding what we love
in common
            making good
with work and celebration
                        charged
to go out unprepared into the world

and take our place for granted
                            every time
we drive back through the slowly dimming fields
to quiet rooms
            and prayers that stay unanswered.

THE IDEA OF HOUSES

I sold my earrings at the gold store to buy a silver ring in the market. I swapped that for old ink and a black notebook. This was before I forgot my pages on the seat of a train that was supposed to take me home. Whenever I arrived in a city, it seemed my home was in a different one.

Olga says, without my having told her any of this, 'Your home is never really home until you sell it. Then you discover all the things you could do with the garden and the big rooms – as if seeing it through the eyes of a broker. You've stored your nightmares in the attic and now you have to pack them in a suitcase or two at best.' Olga goes silent then smiles suddenly, like a queen among her subjects, there in the kitchen between her coffee machine and a window with a view of flowers.

Olga's husband wasn't there to witness this regal episode. Maybe this is why he still thinks the house will be a loyal friend when he goes blind – a house whose foundations will hold him steady and whose stairs, out of mercy, will protect him from falls in the dark.

I'm looking for a key that always gets lost in the bottom of my handbag, where neither Olga nor her husband can see me drilling myself in reality so I can give up the idea of houses.

Every time you go back home with the dirt of

the world under your nails, you stuff everything you were able to carry with you into its closets. But you refuse to define home as the future of junk – a place where dead things were once confused with hope. Let home be that place where you never notice the bad lighting, let it be a wall whose cracks keep growing until one day you take them for doors.

HOME

Homes have no walls
no rooms, no furniture, no thresholds
Nothing through which you might enter
and nothing from which you might want to exit
Because homes are not houses
Homes are built in the eyes
Erected by naked, hungry hearts
In skies, in dew drops, lichen, mosses,
Sometimes on parched, parted lips
Sometimes inside the darkening irises of your eyes
Homes are tender assembles of empty air
Sorted by the linear breaths you lend to me;
Built for unborn little feet to run
And for smiles to sun themselves on broad porticos
My home is in the centre of your palms
Sunk in the wells of your destiny
That you carry like a liquid in your eyes
Or like an abode in your hand, my very own delta
Between the nine mounds of the universe

HOME SUITE

Home is the first
and final poem
and every poem between
has this mum home seam.

Home's the weakest enemy
as iron steams starch –
but to war against home
is the longest march.

Home has no neighbours.
They are less strong
than the tree, or the sideboard.
All who come back belong.

No later first-class plane
flies the sad quilt wings.
Any feeling after final
must be home, with idyll-things.

Love may be recent,
and liquid enough term
to penetrate and mollify
what's compact in home.

LOVE AFTER LOVE

The time will come
when, with elation,
you will greet yourself arriving
at your own door, in your own mirror,
and each will smile at the other's welcome,

and say, sit here. Eat.
You will love again the stranger who was your self.
Give wine. Give bread. Give back your heart
to itself, to the stranger who has loved you

all your life, whom you ignored
for another, who knows you by heart.
Take down the love letters from the bookshelf,

the photographs, the desperate notes,
peel your own image from the mirror.
Sit. Feast on your life.

DEREK WALCOTT (1930–2017)   275

'I DWELL IN POSSIBILITY –'

I dwell in Possibility –
A fairer House than Prose –
More numerous of Windows –
Superior – for Doors –

Of Chambers as the Cedars –
Impregnable of eye –
And for an everlasting Roof
The Gambrels of the Sky –

Of Visitors – the fairest –
For Occupation – This –
The spreading wide my narrow Hands
To gather Paradise –

WORDS IN THE AIR

The clear air said: 'I was your home once
but other guests have taken your place;
where will you go who liked it here so much?
You looked at me through the thick dust
of the earth, and your eyes were known to me.
You sang sometimes, you even whispered low
to someone else who was often asleep,
you told her the light of the earth
was too pure not to point a direction
which somehow avoided death. You imagined
yourself advancing in that direction;
but now I no longer hear you. What have you done?
Above all, what is your lover going to think?'

And she, his friend, replied through tears of
        happiness:
'He has changed into the shade that pleased him best.'

PHILIPPE JACCOTTET (1925–2021)
TR. DEREK MAHON

THE GUEST HOUSE

This being human is a guest house.
Every morning a new arrival.

A joy, a depression, a meanness,
some momentary awareness comes
as an unexpected visitor.

Welcome and entertain them all!
Even if they're a crowd of sorrows,
who violently sweep your house
empty of its furniture,
still, treat each guest honorably.
He may be clearing you out
for some new delight.

The dark thought, the shame, the malice,
meet them at the door laughing,
and invite them in.

Be grateful for whoever comes,
because each has been sent
as a guide from beyond.

RUMI (1207–73)
278   TR. COLEMAN BARKS

I was passionate,
filled with longing,
I searched
far and wide.

But the day
that the Truthful One
found me,
I was at home.

LAL DED (14th century)
TR. JANE HIRSHFIELD

THE HOUSE OF GOD

From a sermon preached on 29th February 1628

And those that sleep in Jesus Christ (saith the
Apostle) will God bring with him . . . They shall
awake as Jacob did, and say as Jacob said, Surely
the Lord is in this place, and this is no other but
the house of God, and the gate of heaven. And into
that gate they shall enter, and in that house they
shall dwell, where there shall be no Cloud nor Sun,
no darkness nor dazzling, but one equal light; no
noise nor silence, but one equal music; no fears nor
hopes, but one equal possession; no foes nor friends,
but one equal communion and identity; no ends nor
beginnings, but one equal eternity.

JOHN DONNE (1572–1631)   279

ENVOI: *HOME*

Here is a thing my heart wishes the world had more of:
I heard it in the air of one night when I listened
To a mother singing softly to a child restless and angry in
the darkness.

CARL SANDBURG (1878–1967)